MW00460006

Proofreading
Secrets
of
Best-Selling
Authors

Kathy Ide

Lighthouse Publishing
of the Carolinas
www.lighthousepublishingofthecarolinas.com

PROOFREADING SECRETS OF BEST-SELLING AUTHORS
BY KATHY IDE
Published by Lighthouse Publishing of the Carolinas
2333 Barton Oaks Dr., Raleigh, NC 27614

ISBN 978-1-938499-34-0
Copyright © 2014 by Kathy Ide
Cover design by Ted Ruybal, www.wisdomhousebooks.com

Available in print from your local bookstore, online, or from the publisher at:
www.lighthousepublishingofthecarolinas.com.

For more information on this book and the author, visit www.KathyIde.com.

Unless otherwise noted, all Scripture quotations are taken from the New King James Version®. Copyright © 1982 by Thomas Nelson, Inc. Used by permission. All rights reserved.

Scripture quotations marked NLT are taken from the Holy Bible, New Living Translation, copyright ©1996, 2004, 2007 by Tyndale House Foundation. Used by permission of Tyndale House Publishers, Inc., Carol Stream, Illinois 60188. All rights reserved.

Brought to you by the creative team at
Lighthouse Publishing of the Carolinas:
Eddie Jones, Rowena Kuo, Meaghan Burnett, and Brian Cross

Library of Congress Cataloging-in-Publication Data
Ide, Kathy.
Proofreading Secrets of Best-Selling Authors / Kathy Ide 1st ed.

Printed in the United States of America.

Much of the material referred to in this book has been drawn from *The Chicago Manual of Style, The Christian Writer's Manual of Style,* and *The Associated Press Stylebook.* Cross-references to CMOS, CWMS, and AP are provided for your convenience. Be sure to consult these reference books (or their online versions) for a more comprehensive treatment of the topics covered here.

ENDORSEMENTS

Polishing the PUGS: Punctuation, Usage, Grammar, and Spelling Tips for Writers contained a lot of the material that is now in sections 2–5 of this book. Here's what some people said about that publication.

Don't buy a copy of Kathy Ide's "PUGS" book!

That's right. Don't buy a copy. Buy two copies: one for yourself and one for someone you'd like to help.

Grammar/punctuation books abound by the hundreds. Kathy's offers a service that's invaluable. She cites *The Chicago Manual of Style*. Every time Kathy gives a rule or principle, she cites the CMOS reference.

I wonder how many people realize what an invaluable service she's offering.

I have two popular style books on my desk. Both of them make statements without backing them up. I prefer to have the backing of CMOS on every bit of editing I do.

Please take my advice: ***Buy at least two copies.*** Someone else will be glad you did.

  —Cecil Murphey, author and coauthor of more than 130 books
     (at last count)

I cannot possibly recommend Kathy's book strongly enough! I hazard to guess that 95 percent of the questions one has about punctuation, usage, grammar, and spelling are covered here. It's so easy to grab the book from the side of my computer, find what I'm looking for in the Table of Contents, and have an answer to my question—in *seconds.*

  —Amber Ferguson, freelance author and editor

Kathy Ide's book is a result of her knowledge of the subject and thorough research. Her love for the language and for writing is evident. This resource will be a favorite for writers, editors, teachers, and everyone else who enjoys words.

—Pam Pugh, Moody Publishers

Kathy Ide's book is a fantastic resource for writers—sort of a "best of" everything: *The Chicago Manual of Style*, Strunk's *Elements of Style*, and other standard manuals on writing, all compiled into one easy reference spot. It is concise, well researched, and conveniently organized, and I refer to it often. My favorite feature is the blank space at the end of each section for you to make notes about your own pet PUGS peeves. I've already added several spelling words to the blank space in the "commonly misspelled words" section. With this book, everything is at your fingertips in a well-organized fashion. I predict I'll wear out my copy within the year.

—Deborah Raney, award-winning novelist

This book is an essential tool for writers and editors. I've read it from cover to cover and still refer to it often. It's a concise guide to great grammar, using *The Chicago Manual of Style* as its basis. I wouldn't be without it.

—Linda Harris, freelance writer and editor

Kathy Ide's book is a practical, concise, and extremely user-friendly reference guide that has made my life easier as both a writer and editor. Not only has it been an invaluable tool in my personal life, but as a mentor to new writers and teacher at writers' conferences, I recommend it to everyone as a *must-have*. This book was the first reference book I purchased as a writer/editor and I simply could not live without it.

—Andrea Merrell, freelance writer and editor

I've been writing for many years, and I've learned a lot through my writing and critique groups that I didn't pick up in my English classes. But with this book, Kathy has put together information that I'm going to treasure with my Strunk and White.

—Gloria Clover, freelance author and editor

I have been writing, editing, and proofreading professionally since 1976. Kathy Ide's wonderful book is worth so very much. She has addressed issues that I have not seen covered elsewhere, and I am extremely familiar with many style/grammar books. Her examples and explanations are some of the best I have encountered. I cannot recommend it enough.

—Marilyn A. Anderson, freelance editor and writer

Kathy Ide's book was helpful when I first began freelance editing seven years ago. Her straightforward, no-nonsense way of putting it together helped me find what I needed, without fuss or aggravation. Since I edit for newsletters as well as book authors, I was particularly glad to see Kathy included both *The Associated Press Stylebook* and *The Chicago Manual of Style* when providing punctuation, usage, grammar, and spelling information.

—Nanette Thorsen-Snipes, freelance editor and writer

Kathy's thoughtful book provides welcome relief for writers and editors who seek a quick reference guide to the most common points of confusion regarding punctuation, usage, grammar, and spelling. Kathy's writing style is fresh and engaging, not an easy tone to project in a reference book.

While I own the latest edition of *The Chicago Manual of Style*, I turn first to Kathy's book. It's faster and easier to manage, and almost always answers my question.

—Sheila Seiler Lagrand, blogger, author, and editor

ACKNOWLEDGMENTS

I'd like to thank my editing clients—aspiring writers, established authors, traditional publishing houses, subsidy publishers, and magazines—for inspiring me to strive for excellence ... and to research the appropriate rules in the industry-standard reference books.

I also deeply appreciate my family members who patiently put up with my quirks and idiosyncrasies—like refusing to follow a truck that had an advertisement with *its'* on it ... and complaining that big national companies ought to hire ad agencies that know when *everyday* should be spelled as two words ... and praising the local grocery store for having express-lane signs that say, "Ten Items or *Fewer*."

Thanks also to my writing colleagues, who have peppered me with questions about punctuation, usage, grammar, and spelling (which I came to call "PUGS"), then raved about how much I knew on these subjects (apparently not realizing that I merely knew where to look up the right answers), and affectionately dubbed me "the PUGS lady." And thanks to all the conference directors and attendees who have allowed me to speak on such a boring-sounding topic and make it fun.

Thanks to my friends who cringe whenever they write me an e-mail because they're sure I'll notice their errors ... but click Send anyway.

A special note of appreciation goes out to my wonderful agent, Diana Flegal, who caught the vision for the projects I had a passion for—even this book, with its unique, targeted readership—and championed them on my behalf.

Finally, I wish to express my deep gratitude to God, my heavenly Father, who has blessed me with such wonderful and understanding friends, family members, clients, and colleagues. And to His Son, my Lord and Savior, Jesus Christ, for giving His all so that I can have assurance of eternal life with Him ... whether my manuscripts are free of mistakes or not.

Table of Contents

Section 1

Proofreading for Typos,
Inaccuracies, and Inconsistencies

Section 2

Punctuation

Section 3

Usage

Section 4

Grammar

Section 5

Spelling

RESOURCES

The Chicago Manual of Style. The University of Chicago Press, Chicago, IL 60637. Copyright © 1969, 1982, 1993, 2003, 2010 by The University of Chicago.

Merriam-Webster's Collegiate® Dictionary, Eleventh Edition. Copyright © 2003 by Merriam-Webster, Inc.

Webster's New World College Dictionary, Fourth Edition. Copyright © 2002 by Wiley Publishing, Inc.

The Christian Writer's Manual of Style. Robert Hudson. Copyright © 2004 by the Zondervan Corporation.

The Associated Press Stylebook and Briefing on Media Law. Darrell Christian, Sally Jacobsen, and David Minthorn, eds. Copyright © 2013 by The Associated Press.

Merriam-Webster's Dictionary of English Usage. Merriam-Webster. Copyright © 1994 by Merriam-Webster, Inc.

Grammatically Correct: The Essential Guide to, Spelling, Style, Usage Grammar, and Punctuation. Anne Stilman. Copyright © 2010 by Writer's Digest Books.

Dictionary of Problem Words and Expressions. Harry Shaw. Copyright © 1987 by McGraw-Hill Inc.

INTRODUCTION

"And what do you do for a living, Mrs. Ide?" The physician's assistant poised his fingers over the keyboard, ready to type my answer in the New Patient form.

"I'm an author and editor."

His bored expression transformed into one of keen interest. With a sparkle in his eyes, he said, "You know..."

Oh, yes, I knew what he was about to say. I'd heard the same response countless times when people learned of my profession.

"I've always wanted to write a book. But I've never been very good at spelling and grammar and all that stuff."

I nodded. "You know, I've always wanted to be a surgeon. But I've never been very good at biology and anatomy and all that stuff." Oh, how I wanted to say that. But I held my tongue and simply smiled.

Many people want to write a book—or at least they think they do. What most people really want is to *have written* a book. They don't realize all the time, effort, and hard work that goes into such an endeavor.

These days, it's easier than ever to get a book published. Self-publishing, subsidy publishing, e-book publishing. Anyone can write just about anything and get it in print or on a mobile device with a little investment of time and money.

But if you want people (besides your family and friends) to *buy* your book, to pay for what you've written, you have to do it well. Really well.

There are many ways to learn professional writing techniques. Read books on how to write. Take classes, courses, workshops, seminars. Attend writers' conferences. Work with a critique partner or group. Hire a freelance editor/mentor.

But once you've learned how to write well, you'll be ready to confidently send your manuscript to a subsidy publisher or submit it to an agent or commercial publisher...right?

Not quite.

Before you submit that piece you've worked so hard on, it's important to give it a final polish. To catch all those annoying typos that slipped in while you were creating your masterpiece. To make sure all the formatting is consistent. That the sentences are punctuated correctly, the grammar is accurate, and the words are spelled right and used right.

"Why bother with that sort of thing?" you may ask. "As long as readers know what I mean, does it really matter whether there's a typo here and there, a comma in the wrong place, or a few words misspelled?"

Yeah. It does.

Literary agent Richard Curtis once wrote:

> It was not long ago that the prevailing attitude among editors was, "This book has some problems, but the author is so talented that I'd like to buy it and work with him." Today such words are rarely heard. A book with problems is a book rejected.[1]

That was written in 2001. Such words are even rarer now than they were then. Acquisitions editors receive so many manuscripts from so many authors these days, they can afford to reject them for the most minuscule reasons.

---

[1] Richard Curtis, interview in *The Christian Communicator,* June 2001.

The October 2004 issue of *Write to the Heart* (the newsletter of the American Christian Fiction Writers) revealed the top pet peeves of nine acquisitions editors from major Christian publishing houses. One said that her main pet peeve was "sloppy manuscripts full of grammatical errors."

Why make such a big deal out of the little things? Because if there are too many mistakes in a manuscript, the message in that nonfiction book or the story of that novel may get lost or even misunderstood. And readers today have so many options, it's easier than ever to simply stop reading one book and move on to another.

OK. So how can you make sure your manuscript is as error-free as possible?

That's where this book comes in.

Proofreading Secrets of Best-Selling Authors reveals tips from multi-published writers on how to catch typos, how to ensure consistency throughout a manuscript (or series), what industry-standard reference books the publishers use, how to punctuate sentences properly, what kinds of words to look up in a dictionary (and which dictionary to use), and more.

Carefully proofreading your manuscript won't guarantee that you'll end up with a best seller. But if you proofread like a best-selling author does, you'll be one step closer...to whatever type of "success" God has in mind for your writing.

About Me

So, who am I to be offering this kind of advice?

I have been a published author since 1989. I've written books, magazine articles, play and movie scripts, short stories, curriculum, and devotionals. I've been a member of several writers' groups over the years, both in person and online. And I've attended numerous writers' conferences across the country.

I have been a full-time freelance editor/proofreader since 1998. I've worked with new writers, established authors, commercial publishing houses, and subsidy publishers. I mentor aspiring writers, taking them from "I've never had anything published, so I don't even know if I have what it takes, but I have a passion in my heart to write and I want to learn how to do it right" to landing an agent, getting a book contract, and seeing their work in print. Many of my clients have successfully self-published books. Several have won awards and contests. Some have become best-selling authors in the CBA (Christian Booksellers Association) and/or the ABA (American Booksellers Association).

I am also the founder and director of The Christian PEN: Proofreaders and Editors Network and the Christian Editor Connection And I speak at several writers' conferences every year.

My familiarity with the publishing industry's reference books began when I started proofreading for publishers. If something didn't look right to me, I wasn't allowed to simply change it to whatever I thought was correct. If I marked a revision to the galleys, I had to make a notation in the margin stating which reference manual I found the correct spelling or punctuation rule in, and what section or page number applied.

I found myself looking up many of the same words and rules repeatedly, so I started a "cheat sheet" for myself. As this list grew, I shared it with other writers and editors, and they found it so helpful I printed copies and put them in a binder. Then I self-published the book and sold it to clients, colleagues, and writers' conference attendees. Their input helped me determine what content would be most beneficial and which examples were most clearly understood.

After years of this "market research," I added a section of proofreading tips from some of the best-selling authors I've had the privilege of coming to know. The result is a cornucopia of ideas to help you catch every typo, inconsistency, inaccuracy, and "PUGS" mistake that may be hiding in your manuscript.

So if you want your writing to be the best it can be ... whether you become a best-selling author or not...this book is for you.

And if you want to proofread other writers' manuscripts—for free or for pay—this book is definitely for you!

REFERENCE BOOKS

Ready for the first *secret* of best-selling authors? It's knowing which reference books are used by the publishers you want to submit your writing to.

There are many punctuation and grammar books on the market, but the standard used by US book publishers is *The Chicago Manual of Style*. (Most publishing houses have their own style guides, which may include a few exceptions to the CMOS rules ... but you won't know that until you get hooked up with a particular house.)

There are several dictionaries out there, too, and strangely enough, they don't always agree on the spellings of all words. The standard for US book publishers is *Merriam-Webster's Collegiate Dictionary*.

Supplemental to these references, most Christian book publishers rely on *The Christian Writer's Manual of Style* for details that are not fully covered in the secular publications.

Unfortunately, reference books sometimes contradict one another. This is the general order of authority:

1. The publisher's in-house style guide

2. *The Chicago Manual of Style* for punctuation and grammar

3. *Merriam-Webster's Collegiate Dictionary* for spelling and usage

4. *The Christian Writer's Manual of Style* for issues directly related to religious matters

5. *The Elements of Style*

Note: For spelling issues, *Merriam-Webster's Collegiate Dictionary* usually trumps *The Chicago Manual of Style*; however, since the current edition of *The Chicago Manual of Style* (2010) is much more recent than the latest edition of Webster's Collegiate (2003), an exception is made for modern terms, such as *website*.

If you write book-length manuscripts, I strongly encourage you to purchase a copy of the most recent edition of each of these reference books.

The Chicago Manual of Style is more than a thousand pages long and can be somewhat intimidating until you get used to it, so I will summarize in this book some of the common problem areas I've come across in my work with authors, publishers, and other freelance editors. For each rule, I've included the abbreviation "CMOS," along with the section number, so you can look up the in-depth explanation in *The Chicago Manual of Style* (16th edition, © 2010). I reference page numbers with the abbreviation "CWMS" for *The Christian Writer's Manual of Style* (© 2004). *The Associated Press Stylebook* doesn't have rule numbers or section numbers, and it is revised every year, so the page numbers are different in every edition. Therefore, I haven't provided page numbers for AP here.

This book is not intended to replace the industry-standard style guides. The Spelling and Usage sections contain brief lists of words you might not think to look up, but that doesn't mean you don't need to purchase the appropriate dictionary. In the same way, while I touch on some punctuation highlights from *The Chicago Manual of Style*, you should consider this book a basic introduction to the official style manual, and be sure to get a copy for your own use.

What about Articles?

Many popular-style magazines use the same references that book publishers do. However, if you write articles for newspapers or journalistic-style magazines, the standard reference books are *The Associated Press Stylebook* and *Webster's New World College Dictionary* (the official dictionary of The Associated Press). For religious terms, the AP stylebook recommends the *Handbook of Denominations in the United States* and the *World Christian Encyclopedia*.

For Articles

I have inserted notes in text boxes like this wherever *The Associated Press Stylebook* ("AP" in the text) differs from *The Chicago Manual of Style* and when *Webster's New World College Dictionary* differs from *Merriam-Webster's Collegiate Dictionary*.

Note that not all discrepancies are pointed out here. And AP updates their stylebook every year (and their online version repeatedly during the year). So when in doubt, check their latest edition (or get the online version).

How about Online Writing?

Web Style Guide is the standard for online publications. It is available online at www.webstyleguide.com. The rules aren't much different, other than for special characters and some formatting.

Why Do I Find Mistakes in Published Books?

As you study the industry-standard references, you may occasionally notice that a book put out by a reputable publisher contains some things that don't follow the rules. The reason for this discrepancy could be one of three things:

1. No book is going to be perfect, no matter how many proofreaders have gone over it.

2. Books that came out prior to the current editions of *The Chicago Manual of Style* and *Merriam-Webster's Collegiate Dictionary* would have followed the rules in the versions that were available at that time.

3. Each publishing house has its own "house style"—certain exceptions to the industry-standard reference books, things they've decided they want to do that deviate from the norm. (If you have a contract with a publisher, and you get a copy of their style guide, you should follow it. Otherwise, use the industry standards. Publishers have no problem taking a manuscript that follows the appropriate reference books and adjusting it to fit their own house rules.)

TEN REASONS TO PROOFREAD
LIKE A BEST-SELLING AUTHOR

Why should you bother proofreading your manuscript for typos, inaccuracies, and inconsistencies, and learning all the rules about punctuation, usage, grammar, and spelling?

1. Mechanical errors can decrease your chance of acceptance by a traditional publisher.

You may think that as long as you've got good content in your nonfiction manuscript, or a good story with lots of conflict and interesting characters in your fiction manuscript, that should be enough. And yes, content and story are very important. But no matter how good those things are, if you have too many mistakes in your manuscript, it may not go any farther than the acquisitions editor's desk.

2. Mechanical errors can cause miscommunication.

A colleague of mine recently sent me an e-mail about a local writers' conference, asking if I'd be on board for it. I responded that I would definitely be on board, especially since it was close to my home. When I reread her e-mail later, I realized she had asked if I was interested in being on *the* board! I gulped. That's a whole different ballgame. I was certainly "on board" with the idea. But serving on "*the* board" would require a significant investment of my time—something that's always in limited supply for me.

I quickly decided the Lord must have wanted me to accept the invitation, and that He allowed me to misread the e-mail so I wouldn't say no without even considering (or praying about) it. And I have thoroughly enjoyed being on *the* board for this exciting conference.

This is an example of reader error, not author mistake. But it does point out how one little missed word can change the entire meaning of a sentence.

3. Mechanical errors can cause confusion.

My older son, Tom, is a very busy professional, and even before he moved out of my home, a lot of our communication took place via e-mail. One Sunday, I asked him what he wanted me to make for dinner that evening. His response was: "When you decide what you can say I decided this and if it's not OK that's OK." It took me a while to decipher it. And when I asked my son for permission to quote that, his response was, "Did I write that? What on earth does it mean?" Even *he* didn't know! Well, after reading that line several times, I came up with this: "When you decide what, you can say, 'I decided this,' and if it's not OK, that's OK." Pretty confusing without the punctuation, isn't it?

4. Mechanical errors can give an unprofessional appearance to publishers and readers.

Most acquisitions editors know a lot about proper punctuation, usage, grammar, and spelling. Most people on publishing committees know a lot about "PUGS" too. You don't want them looking at your manuscript and thinking, *This author has some good things to say, but she doesn't know a comma from a semicolon.*

Even if your manuscript has already been accepted by a traditional publishing house, if their in-house editor has to spend all her time fixing your mistakes, she won't be able to catch the deeper, more subtle nuances of your text. Besides, you won't be presenting a very polished, professional image to your publisher.

5. Mechanical errors can be embarrassing.

A friend of mine once picked up a book at a bookstore and noticed a typo on the back cover. When she reported it to our critique group, she didn't say she'd found a mistake on a book published by "XYZ Publishers." She said she found the mistake on a "Jane Doe" novel. She didn't connect the error to the publishing house, but to the author.

6. Mechanical errors may cause readers to take you and your message less seriously.

Ireland On-Line ran an article on their website on November 15, 2004, with this title: "Crowe Turns Hero to Help Snake Bite Boy." The story was about actor Russell Crowe helping a boy who'd been bitten by a snake. But by spelling *snakebite* as two words, this sentence implies that Mr. Crowe helped a snake bite a boy! Now, I got a good laugh out of that. But I sure don't want those kinds of mistakes showing up in my own writing.

And take a look at this headline: "Rachael Ray finds inspiration in cooking her family and her dog." An image of a *Tails* magazine cover featuring the celebrity chef and that jaw-dropping teaser went viral on Facebook. The magazine cover turned out to be a fake done with Photoshop, but that's a great illustration of how a missing comma can turn a serious piece of writing into a joke.

7. Mechanical errors can affect the sales of your book.

Readers who find a lot of mistakes in your book will not be as likely to recommend that book to their friends. And who knows? You may have a high school English teacher reading your book, and she just might recommend it to her students...unless there are a lot of mistakes in it.

8. Mechanical errors could cost you money.

If you decide to hire someone to edit or proofread your manuscript, and you haven't corrected your punctuation, usage, grammar, and spelling, you will be paying extra for someone else to do that for you. And how will you know if that editor is right?

9. Mechanical errors can be distracting.

If I'm reading a book or article, no matter how good the content or story might be, if there are too many typos or mistakes in punctuation, usage, grammar, or spelling, it's difficult for me to get past those enough to concentrate on the book. I often stop reading a book and put it back on the shelf when I come across too many errors. And there are other readers like me out there.

10. Mechanical errors can give you a poor reputation.

If you self-publish, or work with a small, independent publisher that doesn't proofread carefully, your book may go out to the public with several typos, inconsistencies, or PUGS errors. Readers who catch those mistakes may consider you an amateur.

For a lot of avid readers, typos practically jump off the page. And many are familiar with the rules of punctuation, usage, grammar, and spelling. If your reader finds mistakes that you missed, that's not going to make you look very good.

Representing the Lord

Christian authors have an added reason to produce writing that is as error-free as possible. Some people refuse to read Christian books because they don't think they're as well written as those published by the mainstream presses. A well-proofread book will reflect positively on you, your faith, and your God.

Details Are Important

How much time and effort have you put into the other aspects of your writing? Is your manuscript not worth proofreading? If your craft was pottery, would you go to the effort of creating a beautiful pot and then not glaze it? If you were a carpenter, would you build a coffee table and not stain and varnish it? If you made an afghan, would you not tie off the last row? If you sewed a garment, would you not finish the seams and hems?

And if you did create something without finishing it properly, would you put out your unfinished craft for sale to strangers, expecting people to pay you for it?

Professionalism Is Key

I love to sing, and my voice sounds delightful when I'm alone in my car with the radio blaring and the windows rolled up. But I wouldn't dream of asking someone to pay to hear me belt out a tune. Not without taking some serious singing lessons.

If you're writing just for family and friends, it may not matter so much whether every comma is in exactly the right place or if you have a few typos here and there. But if you want to get your book published in today's highly competitive commercial market, you need every edge you can get. If you expect people to buy what you write, you need to take the time to do it right.

A Writer's Tools

Words and punctuation marks are the tools of a writer's trade. It is important for you to learn how to use your tools properly.

That's what this book is all about. Consider it an "owner's manual" for the tools you use in your writing every day.

Section 1

Proofreading for Typos, Inaccuracies, and Inconsistencies

TYPOS

What Is a Typo?

One example of a typo is a mistyped word. Running spell-check can catch some typos. But all too often, a mistyped word is a correctly spelled word, just not the right one.

Missing words, or words that shouldn't be there, and words that are in the incorrect order are also typos. And the spell-checker won't catch those.

Missing punctuation is also considered a typo; for example, if you have an open quotation mark but no closing quotation mark. Or there's no punctuation at the end of a sentence.

If you forgot to indent a paragraph, or you indented one paragraph more or less than the others, or if there's a blank space between paragraphs, those are typos too.

Text or punctuation that's in bold or italics that shouldn't be is also a typo. This can happen if you've cut and pasted. Or if you've realized something should not be in bold or italics, and you fixed it, but you missed a little part, like a period or quotation mark or parenthesis.

If you've centered a line of text, like a chapter heading, and your word-processing program has a left indent on that line, the text is not properly centered. That's also a typo.

Catching Typos

Of course, you don't want obvious mistakes showing up in your writing. But since the human eye tends to see what the mind expects to see, catching your own typos can be difficult.

So how do you prevent them? Here are a few suggestions from some of the best-selling authors I've had the privilege of getting to know during my years in the publishing industry. (See Appendix B for their bios.)

Use spell-check, but don't count on it.

New York Times best-selling author Cindy Woodsmall offers this tip:

> Keep the automatic spell-check turned on, regardless of your skill level of editing. Even though you can't rely on it to catch every misspelled word or any homonyms, it will find a good many typos.

Read your manuscript out loud.

Gayle Roper says, "Rhythm issues, repeated words, and awkward phraseology suddenly jump off the page when you read your manuscript out loud."

"I read everything I write out loud," Renae Brumbaugh told me. "That forces me to slow down and look at each word. I find improvements for cadence and style as well as catch grammar and typing errors."

Have someone else read the manuscript to you.

Susan Meissner says that having someone read your manuscript to you will help you catch those "pet words" that you've repeated too many times and/or too close together.

Gail Gaymer Martin adds:

> Listening to my book helps me catch typos, awkward or unclear sentences, lack of rhythm, and redundancy. If you don't have someone who can do that for you, NaturalReader is an excellent tool.

NaturalReader is a text-to-speech software program that can read to you from Microsoft Word files, web pages, PDFs, and e-mails. It has both male and female voices.

Nuance makes a speech-recognition software called Dragon that enables you to use your voice to create documents, send e-mails, search the web, etc. This program also has a function that reads back to you. It has multiple versions for different prices.

Let the manuscript sit for a few days.

"I try to never submit a piece the same day I wrote it," says Renae Brumbaugh, "no matter how good I think it is. I step back from it for a day or two, then reread. I almost always find something to improve."

Kathi Macias adds:

> Nothing works better for me than getting away from a manuscript for a minimum of one week. Then I can read it with "fresh eyes." I get alone someplace where I know I won't have any interruptions and read it with red pen in hand. It's amazing the things I catch!

Kay Marshall Strom suggests letting a manuscript "cool" for at least a week.

Print out your manuscript.

"Don't rely on reading on-screen," warns Deborah Raney. "For some reason, the eye catches things on paper that it glides right past on the computer."

Proofread backward.

Lena Nelson Dooley recommends "starting on the last page and going backward" through the whole manuscript.

Lynette Sowell advises:

> Start at the last sentence of the chapter you've written, and work your way backward, reading each sentence until you get to the beginning. Sometimes the brain can fool you into thinking you know what comes next, because your eye "wants" to see what you "know" you've written.

Take your time.

Anita Higman suggests:

> Avoid bulldozing through in one or two sessions, since the faster you go the more likely you are to miss some errors. Give the process some breathing room. You'll be glad you did—and so will your editor!

Wanda Brunstetter says: "With each set of edits, I go line by line, looking for things like redundancies, wordiness, too much detail, and making sure adjectives and adverbs are not overused."

Proofreading in sections can also be beneficial. For fiction, read only the dialogue, then go back and read only the narrative. Read one character's dialogue and actions, then another character's dialogue and actions. For nonfiction, check just the headings, then the first paragraphs of each section, the second paragraphs, etc. If you're not reading in context, you're more likely to catch the typos as well as inconsistencies.

Try reading one word at a time. Point to each word with your finger as you go. At this stage, work on just a page or two at a time. The longer you sit and read, the more likely you are to miss a mistake.

Have someone else look at it.

It's always easier to find someone else's typos than your own, because you know what you meant.

Mary DeMuth says: "After taking a month off, I look at my manuscript again, edit it, then give it to my critique partners to do a final once-over. Then I go through the book again to make sure I've covered all my bases."

Of course, if you ask people to proofread your manuscript, don't forget to offer to do the same for them in return.

I heartily concur with all of these suggestions. I thoroughly proofread the content of this book multiple times, and so did a lot of other people (including professional editors and proofreaders). Since this is a book about proofreading, I wanted it to be as close to mistake-free as possible. So prior to sending it to the publisher, I printed it out... and was stunned at the errors I found. I fixed them, printed it again, and couldn't believe how many mistakes I still needed to correct!

When I asked a few colleagues (fellow freelance editors) to look over what I thought was my final manuscript, they found errors I'd missed too.

After all that proofreading, I hope you don't discover any typos in this book. But if you do, please e-mail me (Kathy@KathyIde.com). I'll want to get them fixed before the next printing!

INACCURACIES

Research everything in your manuscript. If you have stated facts or presented statistics in your nonfiction book, make sure you've quoted them accurately (and properly cited the original sources).

In fiction, everything your characters do or say needs to be true to life. If your characters live in a different location than you do, have different jobs, hobbies, or interests, or have a different background from yours, make sure they all talk and act the way real people like that would.

Quoting Other Sources

If you have quotations in your manuscript (whether you got them from a book, an article, a blog post, or the Bible), look them all up to make absolutely certain you've copied them *exactly* as in the original—not just the words, but also the spelling, capitalization, and punctuation. Never rely on your memory, no matter how sure you are that you've memorized something accurately.

The Chicago Manual of Style (#2.41, 13.7–8) and *The Christian Writer's Manual of Style* (pp. 258–259, 348, 351–352) allow for the following exceptions when quoting:

1. Single quotation marks may be changed to double, and double to single, as the situation warrants.

2. Commas or periods outside the closing quotation mark may be moved inside.

3. The initial letter may be changed to a capital or a lowercase letter (depending on whether the quote makes a complete thought).

4. Introductory words like *And, Or, For, Therefore, But,* and *Verily* can be omitted.

5. The final punctuation mark in the original quotation may be omitted or changed to suit the format of the sentence in which it is quoted, and punctuation marks may be omitted where ellipsis points are used.

6. In a passage quoted from a modern book, journal, or newspaper, an obvious typographical error may be corrected. (Leave archaic spellings the same.)

7. Words that are italicized in Scripture because they were added by the Bible translator for clarity should not be italicized when a verse or passage is quoted in a manuscript.

8. When quoting a passage of Scripture, do not include the verse numbers (unless the text following the quotation is an analysis of the individual verses).

9. The words *Lord* and *God* should not be written in cap-and-small-cap style (Lord and God), even if printed that way in the original text. (*Exception:* Zondervan, the US publisher of the New International Version, prefers that the cap-and-small-cap format be used for Old Testament uses of Lord. Do not, however, use this format when writing *Lord* or *God* within the text of your manuscript—only in NIV quotations from the OT.)

10. In some Bible translations, certain portions of Scripture have each verse on a separate line, and the first word of each line is capitalized, regardless of whether the word begins a new sentence. When such passages are quoted in a manuscript, the verses do not need to be set as separate paragraphs. If you put them in running text, capitalize only proper names, the first word of a sentence, and the first word of a direct quotation.

Citing Sources

As a matter of ethics, copyright law, and courtesy to readers, make sure you've identified the source of every direct quotation in your manuscript, as well as all facts, statistics, or opinions not universally known or easily verified. (Note: Do not state something as fact simply because you've heard it often quoted—like "Fifty percent of all marriages end in divorce.")

There are three basic styles of documentation: footnotes, endnotes, and bibliography. (See *The Chicago Manual of Style* for details on how to do them properly.)

It is the author's responsibility (not the publisher's) to research and verify the sources of all quotations and to request written permission to quote anything that isn't covered under Fair Use or Public Domain.

Different versions of the Bible have different fair-use guidelines. Make sure you do not quote more than the allowed amount without obtaining proper permission. (See pages 56–73 of *The Christian Writer's Manual of Style* for a list of guidelines for most popular Scripture versions, including where to write to request permission for each one.)

Scripture References

Whenever you use words, phrases, sentences, verses, or passages from Scripture, you need to identify the book of the Bible, chapter, and verse(s)…even if you change the wording slightly. (Use quotation marks around the exact words taken from the text.)

Scripture references are given in numerals, not spelled out. Use a colon between chapter and verse, with no space between (John 3:16), a comma between nonconsecutive verse numbers (John 3:16, 18), and an en dash between consecutive verses (John 3:16–18) or consecutive chapters (Acts 1–3).

In parenthetical references, use a semicolon to differentiate between books of the Bible (Matthew 25:2; Mark 12:6) as well as between chapters (Luke 7:16; 10:4).

List all references within a parenthetical in the order in which they appear in Scripture. If you want to highlight a single verse or passage and also list others, put "see also" or "cf." (which means "compare") after the main one, then list the others in their proper order in the Bible. For example:

> I was found by those who did not seek Me; I was made manifest to those who did not ask for Me. (Romans 10:20; see also Isaiah 65:1)

> Matthew uses the phrase "kingdom of heaven" more often than "kingdom of God" (e.g., Matthew 3:2; 4:17; 5:3; but cf. 6:33; 12:28; 19:24; 21:31, 43).

Books of the Bible in text should always be spelled out (except in scholarly/technical books and reference-type works in which there are numerous Scripture references). When references are in parentheses, books of the Bible may be spelled out or abbreviated at the author's/publisher's discretion, but the same format should be used consistently throughout the manuscript. (See Appendix A for a list of proper abbreviations for books of the Bible.)

The AP stylebook says that books of the Bible should never be abbreviated.

For books of the Bible that start with a number, use Arabic numerals (2 John), not Roman numerals (II John). If it comes at the beginning of a sentence, spell it out ("First Peter 1:3 says ...").

Note: When referencing a single chapter from the book of Psalms (or verses from a single chapter), use the singular form (e.g., "Psalm 101" or "Psalm 23:4"). When referencing multiple chapters, use the plural form (e.g., "Psalms 4–8"). "Proverbs," however, is always plural.

When referring to one or more verses of Scripture, the words *verse* and *verses* should be spelled out in running text. They may be abbreviated in parenthetical references (e.g., "v. 13" or "vv. 16–20") as long as you are consistent throughout the manuscript.

For popular or trade books, do not add a lowercase letter to the verse number to indicate that only a portion of a verse is being quoted. The context usually makes this clear. Only use a letter if several parts of a verse are being examined individually and successively, or if you're writing a scholarly, academic work. (See *The Christian Writer's Manual of Style,* page 359.)

Bible Versions

At the beginning of the manuscript, indicate which Bible version(s) you quoted from within the text. If only one version was used, or one was used predominantly, and you identify it at the beginning, there is no need to identify that version after each quote in the text. If multiple versions are used, identify only the alternate version(s) in the text. Example:

> "Shout with joy to the Lord, all the earth!" (Psalm 100:1 NLT)

If you really want to impress your publisher, include complete copyright notices for each Bible version you used in the front matter of your manuscript. (See the Scripture copyright notices at the front of this book as examples.) These notices can be found at BibleGateway.com and on Bible publishers' websites. They're also printed in the front matter of every Bible.

Note: Do not use the copyright notice for the specific Bible (e.g., study Bibles), just the Scripture *version* you're quoting from.

INCONSISTENCIES

When it comes to punctuation, usage, grammar, and spelling, most things are black and white, right or wrong. But a few things are left up to the author's discretion. In those situations, make sure you've been consistent throughout the manuscript.

Here are some of the things you'll want to check for as you proofread for consistency.

Formatting

Do your best to follow industry-standard formatting guidelines (or, if you're working for a specific publisher, their house-style guidelines) for things like font, font size, paragraph alignment, titles/subtitles, page breaks, etc.

If there's not an industry standard for something, at least make sure you're consistent throughout the manuscript. For example:

- If you decide to center your chapter headings, make sure all chapter headings are centered.

- If you choose to start chapters down six (or eight) lines from the top of the page, start all chapters down six (or eight) lines.

- If you use numerals for chapter numbers, make sure you don't have any chapter numbers spelled out.

- All of your chapter titles should be in the same font, font size, and format (bold, italics, initial caps/all caps/only the first word capped, etc.). Same for all headings and subheadings.

- All chapter titles should be either complete sentences with periods at the end or incomplete sentences without periods. Same for all headings and subheadings.

- Make sure the first line of every paragraph is indented the same amount of space (usually .5 inch) and using the same method (tabs or automatic indent—never use multiple spaces).

- If you use bulleted or numbered lists, make sure they're all indented the same way (first and subsequent lines).

- Headers should be in the same position and the same format on every page of the manuscript. Running page numbers need to be in the same position, too, and they must be consecutive from beginning to end.

- If you use converted fractions (½, ¼, etc.), make sure you don't have any fractions that are not converted (1/2, 1/4, etc.).

- If you use superscripted ordinal numbers (18th, 21st, etc.), make sure all ordinals are superscripted (no 18th, 21st, etc.). Note: Superscripting is not the preferred method according to *The Chicago Manual of Style*. But some publishers prefer them that way.

Punctuation and Capitalization

Today's word-processing programs can convert double hyphens to en dashes and em dashes. We'll be discussing the use of both kinds of dashes later. The point here is that whether you decide to use dashes or hyphens, be consistent throughout. And if you use em dashes, use en dashes too (unless you're following AP style, which doesn't use en dashes).

If you abbreviate books of the Bible in parenthetical references, make sure they're abbreviated in every reference. And make sure to use the proper abbreviations. (See Appendix A.)

Whether you choose to capitalize pronouns for deity or lowercase them, be sure you've been consistent throughout the manuscript.

Fixing Inconsistencies

Here are some common punctuation problems and ways you can easily fix them.

1. More than one space between sentences

Do a find-and-replace, with two spaces in the "find" box and one space in the "replace" box, then click "replace all" until the count gets down to zero.

2. Automatic spacing between paragraphs

Do a "select all," then go to Paragraph/Spacing and put a zero (0) in each of the boxes (for before and after). While you're there, choose either single-spaced or double-spaced (depending on the publisher's preference).

3. Straight apostrophes and quotation marks

The Chicago Manual of Style (#6.112) says that published works should use directional (aka "curly" or "smart") quotation marks and apostrophes. Today's word-processing programs can convert straight apostrophes and quotation marks to directional ones. If that option is selected some of the time you're typing, and not selected other times, you'll end up with inconsistencies. If you copy and paste something from the Internet, like a Scripture passage, it will probably have straight apostrophes and quotation marks.

To make sure these are consistent, check to see that the "smart/curly quotes" option is selected, then use find-and-replace. Type an apostrophe in each box, then click "replace all." Do the same thing for quotation marks.

After you've done that, look for apostrophes that appear at the beginning of a word, because your word-processing program will consider them to be open single quotation marks, which means they'll be curled the wrong direction (for example, 'tis instead of 'tis).

If you have a space or a dash before a closing quotation mark, that will curl the wrong way too (—" instead of —"). Be sure you fix those as well.

Fiction Details

As you proofread your novel manuscript, create a profile for each of your characters to keep track of things like:

- spelling of name/nickname (Seems obvious, but I once proofread a manuscript that had a character's name spelled three different ways.)

- eye color

- hair color, length, and style

- height/build

- date of birth (age at beginning and throughout the story)

- place of birth

- family details (parents, siblings, childhood memories)

- education/training

- hobbies, sports

- face details (freckles, facial hair, complexion)

- quirks

- pet words and phrases used in dialogue (or internal monologue)

- favorite color, food, drink, season, holiday, weather, etc.

- pretty much any detail that comes up in the story

Mary DeMuth says she keeps a little notebook next to her while she's proofreading her novel manuscripts, "to take notes on things like characters' eye color, personality traits, dropped scenes (or scenes that aren't tied up)."

Cindy Woodsmall suggests:

Read as much of the manuscript at one time as possible. Get fully into the story. Let it play out in your head like a movie, and you'll uncover inconsistencies or plot holes that can be fixed before it goes to print. I schedule two eight-hour days back to back. I use sticky notes to jot down any questions that come up and adhere them to the appropriate page.

You may also want to create a timeline, keeping track of the day and date each of your scenes occurs on, to make sure events in your story happen in a realistic manner.

Suzanne Woods Fisher offers this tip that has made a big difference in proofreading her novels:

One of the last things I do before turning in a manuscript is to create a timeline directly out of it—even if I already made one before I began writing. Oh, the errors I catch!

A detailed style sheet is even more important if you're writing a series of novels. Lisa Tawn Bergren recommends keeping track of "every single nuance and detail you note in each successive book, to make sure they stay consistent. It's amazing what you forget in between! Do the same for key dates, births and deaths, and timelines."

Cindy Woodsmall adds:

> If you're writing a series, create bulleted notes on the layout of each main home and property. I label every heading with the last name of the main character who lives there. The goal is to be consistent with your descriptions of the house and surrounding land as well as the distance to the road, the neighbors, or a best friend's home. This would include things like the type of herbs or flowers your character planted on the left side of the house. It sounds trivial, but it'll save you hours of researching your old manuscripts while trying to write a new one.

FINAL STEPS

After you've followed all of the above steps, there are two more things I'd recommend.

Get professional help.

While all this detailed proofreading might make you a little crazy, that's not the kind of "professional help" I'm referring to. After you've done everything you can to polish your manuscript to the best of your ability, consider hiring a freelance proofreader and see if he or she finds anything you missed. (I can almost guarantee you this will happen!)

Now, you'll want to hire someone who's well acquainted with the industry-standard guidelines for the type of writing you do. Don't ask a person who specializes in articles to proofread your book manuscript (or vice versa). Don't have a nonfiction specialist proofread your novel, because there are some subtle but important differences. And please, do not ask your neighbor who teaches college English to proofread your manuscript. Schools don't use the same style guides publishers do. On the other hand, most line-by-line copyeditors make excellent proofreaders. And they may catch more than just typos, inaccuracies, inconsistencies, and PUGS errors in your manuscript.

If you don't know any professional proofreaders or copyeditors, check out the Christian Editor Connection (www.ChristianEditor.com). They can connect you with established, professional freelancers based on your genre, editorial needs, turnaround time, and budget.

Accept that your manuscript will never be perfect.

No matter how painstakingly you proofread your manuscript, or how many other eyes have carefully scrutinized it, a few errors will probably slip through.

For a few years, I proofread galleys for Moody Publishers. This is the final stage before a book goes to print. Each of these manuscripts had already gone through an overall critique, a substantive content edit, and a line-by-line copyedit. Surely the author, her writing partners, and all those professional editors would have caught most of the mistakes, right?

When I started doing this for Moody, I was the *fifth* proofreader. I could hardly believe they would hire five proofreaders. Could I really find anything that all those other professionals missed?

Boy, was I in for a surprise. I was amazed at how many mistakes I found that the four proofreaders before me didn't catch.

Eventually, I worked my way up from fifth proofreader to first. And then I couldn't help wondering how many mistakes I'd miss that the four proofreaders after me would find!

And yet, in spite of all this meticulous attention to detail by so many trained professionals, how often have you read a commercially published book and found one or more errors in it? (I think that's God's way of showing us how imperfect we all are!)

Randy Ingermanson shares this advice from his personal experience:

> Every few years, you get an e-mail from some horribly picky fan who lists every single typo she found in your book. Don't get mad. Thank her profusely, and then ask if she'd be willing to read the manuscript for your next book so you won't be embarrassed by typos in the future. She'll probably be happy to do that, probably for free, and you can thank her in the acknowledgments.

Section 2

Punctuation

Punctuation

Some people think they should be able to put commas and other punctuation marks wherever seems right to them. But the way a sentence is punctuated can affect the meaning. And for writers who want to come across as professionals, it's important to punctuate according to industry-standard guidelines.

That's why, for each section in this chapter, I'll reference rule numbers from *The Chicago Manual of Style* (16th edition) with the abbreviation "CMOS," page numbers from *The Christian Writer's Manual of Style* (2004) with the abbreviation "CWMS," and references to *The Associated Press Stylebook* (2013) with the abbreviation "AP." Be sure to look up each rule in the official reference books for more details.

APOSTROPHES

Possessives
CMOS #7.15–28 and CWMS pp. 306–308

To form the possessive of most *singular* nouns (proper or otherwise), add an apostrophe and an *s*. Examples:

the book's success

a reader's favorite genre

Robert Burns's poems

Charles's manuscript

the business's income

John Williams's plotline

an hour's time

a month's absence

the marquis's territory

Xerxes's throne

Note: The 15th edition of *The Chicago Manual of Style* recommended dropping the *s* after the apostrophe for words and names that end in an unpronounced *s* (like *marquis*) or with an *eez* sound (like *Xerxes*). CMOS-16 does not make this exception.

To form the possessive of *plural* nouns ending in *s*, add an apostrophe only. Examples:

the Williamses' house

the puppies' tails

two weeks' notice

authors' rights

Use apostrophe-*s* if the plural term does not end in *s*. Examples:

women's novels

children's books

For Articles

Use an apostrophe only (no extra *s*) for singular proper names ending in *s*. Examples:

Dickens' novels

Charles' book

Jesus' life

Xerxes' armies

Moses' law

> For singular common nouns ending in *s*, add apostrophe-*s* unless the next word begins with an *s*. Examples:
>
> hostess's invitation
>
> witness' story

The Christian Writer's Manual of Style (p. 307) states that when a name has two *s* sounds in the last syllable, or when the final *s* sounds like a *z*, do not add an *s* after the apostrophe. Examples:

Jesus'

Ramses'

Kansas'

Achilles'

Note: *The Chicago Manual of Style* does not make these exceptions. They prefer adding apostrophe-*s* to all proper names. (Most Christian publishers follow CWMS on this—especially when it comes to dropping the *s* after the apostrophe in the possessive form of *Jesus*.)

Descriptive Phrases
CMOS #7.25 and AP

When a plural noun ending in *s* is used to modify another noun, use an apostrophe without an added *s*. No apostrophe in proper names that do not use one. Examples:

a teachers' college

a writers' conference

writers' guidelines

Publishers Weekly

Diners Club

Plurals
CMOS #7.8, 7.13–14 and CWMS p. 51 and AP

Do not use an apostrophe for most plurals. Examples:

dos and don'ts

no ifs, ands, or buts

the 1980s

the Joneses

maybes

yeses and nos

thank-yous

Molly got three As and two Cs.

five Toms, four Dicks, and three Harrys

I had to go to two DMVs to get my license renewed.

Exception: To avoid confusion, pluralize single lowercase letters by adding apostrophe-*s*. Examples:

> *a*'s and *b*'s
>
> *x*'s and *y*'s

"For...sake" Expressions
CMOS #7.20 and AP

"For...sake" expressions used with a singular noun that ends in *s* get only an apostrophe, no additional *s*. Examples:

> for righteousness' sake
>
> for goodness' sake

For Articles

Use an apostrophe without an *s* for the following expressions:

> for appearance' sake
>
> for conscience' sake
>
> for goodness' sake

To Replace Omitted Letters
CMOS #7.29 and AP

An apostrophe replaces omitted letters in a word. Examples:

readin' and writin'

'tis the season

rock 'n' roll

ne'er-do-well

Years

CMOS #9.31 and CWMS p. 51 and AP

If years are abbreviated to two numerals, they should be preceded by an apostrophe. Example:

Phil's first novel was published in '82.

Note: If you're using "curly quotes," make sure the apostrophe is curled in the right direction ('82, not '82).

ADD YOUR OWN

As you look up rules in *The Chicago Manual of Style*, *The Christian Writer's Manual of Style*, or *The Associated Press Stylebook*, you may find yourself needing to check the same rule over and over. To save yourself time, jot down here anything you think you'll need in the future. Be sure to note the appropriate section so you can look it up again if needed.

My Favorite Apostrophe Rules

Reference Book   Rule or Page #   Rule

CAPITALIZATION

Family Relationships
CMOS #8.35 and CWMS p. 111 and AP

"Kinship names" (father, brother, aunt, cousin, etc.) are lowercased when used generically or when preceded by a modifier. Examples:

> my dad

> the youngest mother in the group

> her aunt Shelly

Kinship names are capitalized when they immediately precede a person's name or are used alone in place of the person's name. Examples:

> I know that Mother's middle name is Marie.

> Does Aunt Courtney have a book signing on Saturday?

> Hey, Son, are we going fishing today or not?

Terms of Endearment
CWMS p. 112 and AP

The 15th edition of CMOS (#8.39) said that terms of affection—aka "pet names" (*honey, dear, sweetheart*)—are always lowercased. AP agrees. CWMS also agrees—unless a term is used so often and consistently that it becomes a person's nickname. CMOS-16 does not include this rule. They now leave it up to author/publisher preference.

Professional Titles
CMOS #8.18–27

Civil, military, religious, academic, government, and professional titles are capitalized when they immediately precede a personal name and are thus part of the name. Titles are lowercased when following a name or used in place of a name. Examples:

> President Washington; the president

> General Patton; the general

> Cardinal Richelieu; the cardinal

> Professor Crawford; the professor

> Governor Johnson; the governor

> Senator John Kerry; the senator from Massachusetts

In promotional or ceremonial contexts (such as a list of donors or corporate officers), titles are capitalized even when following a name. Example:

> Cristina Lopez, Manager of International Sales

A title used in place of a personal name is capitalized in such contexts as a toast or formal introduction, or when used in direct address. Examples:

> Ladies and gentlemen, the Prime Minister.

> But Captain, that man's a stowaway.

Hello, Mr. President.

What's the prognosis, Doctor?

Military Forces
CMOS #8.111

Titles of armies, navies, air forces, etc. are capitalized. Words such as *army* and *navy* are lowercased when standing alone, when used collectively in the plural, or when not part of an official title (even though these terms are often capitalized in official or promotional contexts). Examples:

Confederate army (and Confederate navy)

Union army (American Civil War)

Eighth Air Force; Fifth Army

National Guard

United States (or US) Air Force, Army, Coast Guard, Marine Corps, Navy

the air force, the army, the navy

the Coast Guard or the coast guard

the Marine Corps or the marine corps

a marine

> **For Articles**
>
> Capitalize when referring to U.S. forces (the Air Force, the Army, the Marines, the Navy; Air Force (or Army or Navy) regulations; the Marine Corps).
>
> Lowercase for forces of other nations (e.g., the French army).

Academic Subjects, Courses, and Degrees
CMOS #8.28, 8.84–8.85

Academic subjects are lowercased unless they form part of a department name or an official course name. Examples:

> I majored in contemporary literature.

> I pursued graduate studies in philosophy and science.

> I took a class called Basic Manuscript Editing.

Degrees are capitalized on a résumé, business card, diploma, directory, etc. In running text, names of degrees are lowercased. Examples:

> a master's degree

> a bachelor's degree

> master of business administration

Terms of Respect
CMOS #8.32

Honorific titles are capitalized. But general terms of respect are not. Examples:

His/Her/Your Majesty

His/Her/Your Excellency

His/Her/Your Honor

my lord; my lady

sir; ma'am

Pronouns for God
CMOS #8.94 and CWMS pp. 169–170

The Chicago Manual of Style states that pronouns referring to God, Jesus, or the Holy Spirit are not capitalized. (Note: This changed from the 14th to the 15th edition.) Their reasoning is that these pronouns are lowercased "in most English translations of the Bible."

The Christian Writer's Manual of Style says, "The capitalization of pronouns referring to persons of the Trinity has been a matter of debate for many decades. ... Impassioned arguments have been offered up on both sides of the question." They then cite the policy of Zondervan (US publisher of the New International Version of the Bible), which is: "In most cases, lowercase the deity pronoun."

The reasons given by Zondervan are as follows. (Note: These are excerpts. For a more complete explanation, see pages 169–170 of *The Christian Writer's Manual of Style*.)

Many religious publishers and most general publishers have adopted the lowercase style, in large part to conform to the styles of the most commonly used versions of the Bible (the KJV, the NIV, and the RSV). Because capitalizing the deity pronoun was the predominant style in the late nineteenth- and early twentieth-century publishing, it gives a book, at best, a dated, Victorian feel, and at worst, an aura of irrelevance to modern readers.

Contrary to popular opinion, capitalization is not used in English as a way to confer respect. (We capitalize both God and Satan, Churchill and Hitler.) Capitalization is largely used in English to distinguish specific things from general. Jesus is no more specific, in that sense, than Peter, and both should therefore be referred to as *he*.

CWMS adds, "There are some situations in which the capitalization of deity pronouns is preferred; for instance, in books that have a deliberately old-fashioned tone or when the author quotes extensively from a Bible version that uses the capitalized style."

Here are my personal suggestions:

1. If you're writing for a specific publisher, find out their preference and use that. If you have a strong conviction that differs from the publisher's style, ask if they'll allow the variance.

2. If you're not writing for a particular house, use your own preference, but be consistent throughout the book. (You may have noticed that deity pronouns are capitalized in this book. I did that because some of my clients and colleagues are offended when pronouns for God aren't capitalized, and those who prefer using lowercase deity pronouns don't feel as strongly about it. Fortunately, my publisher allowed me this leeway.)

3. If you quote exclusively (or even predominantly) from a Bible version that capitalizes deity pronouns, do the same in your text. If you quote from a version that lowercases deity pronouns, follow that format. This will make your text look consistent with your quotes.

Tip: If you choose to capitalize pronouns for deity, do *not* capitalize *who, whom, who's,* or *whose.* But *do* capitalize *He, Him, His; You, Your, Yours; Me, My, Mine; Thee, Thou, Thine.* (See CWMS page 170.)

For Articles

The Associated Press Stylebook says to lowercase pronouns referring to the deity.

Regional Terms
CMOS #8.46–8.49 and CWMS p. 111

Regional terms that are considered proper names should be capitalized. Adjectives and generic nouns are not. Examples of capitalized terms:

Central America

the East/North/South/West

East/West Coast (US)

Eastern (when referring to the Orient and Asian culture)
Eastern/Northern/Southern/Western Hemisphere

Eastern Seaboard (US)

Middle East/Eastern

the Midwest (US)

North/South Pole (also, the Pole)

the Northeast/Northwest/Southeast/Southwest

Northern/Southern California (does not apply to other US states)

the South (US)

Upper Michigan

Western world

Examples of lowercased terms:

central Europe

eastern/northern/southern/western

easterner/westerner

the equator

northern Africa

northerner/southerner (capitalized only in Civil War contexts) oriental culture

polar regions

the south of France

CMOS says that national or geographical names should be lowercased when used with a nonliteral meaning. Examples: *brussels sprouts, dutch oven, french dressing, french fries, roman numerals, swiss cheese.*

Webster's Collegiate lists *Dutch oven, French dressing, Roman numerals,* and *Swiss cheese.* Their listings for *brussels sprouts* and *french fries* say the first words in these phrases are "often capitalized."

Note: Whether you capitalize or lowercase *brussels*, do not leave off the *s* at the end. It's not *brussel sprouts.*

For Articles

The AP stylebook lists *Brussels sprouts, Dutch oven, French dressing, Roman numerals,* and *Swiss cheese,* but *french fries* (because it refers to the style of cut, not the nation).

Webster's New World College Dictionary lists *Brussels sprouts, Dutch oven, French dressing,* and *Roman numerals.* It lists *French fries* (but says the first word is "often" lowercased) and *Swiss cheese* (saying the first word is "sometimes" lowercased).

Topographical Names
CMOS #8.52

Names of mountains, rivers, oceans, and islands are capitalized. When a generic term is used descriptively rather than as part of the name, or if it is used alone, it is lowercased. Examples:

the California desert

the Hawaiian Islands (but "the island of Hawaii")

the Hudson River valley

Capitalize the generic term when it applies to two or more names preceding it. For example, "the Illinois and the Chicago Rivers."

Religious Terms
CMOS #8.90–8.110 and CWMS pp. 121–132

The Christian Writer's Manual of Style has a comprehensive list of which religious terms should be capitalized and which should be lowercased. Here are a few examples from that list.

While *Bible* and *Scripture* and *Messiah* (nouns) are capitalized, *biblical* and *scriptural* and *messianic* (adjectives) are not. Similarly, you would capitalize *the Almighty* (noun) but not *almighty God* (adjective). Capitalize *the One* if you're using that as a title for God, but lowercase that word in phrases such as "the one true God" and "God is the one who …"

The word *apostle* is lowercased, even when used with a person's name (e.g., "the apostle Paul").

The word *church* is only capitalized when referring to the Church of England or the Church of Rome, or when it is part of the official name of a specific church, such as "the First Baptist Church of Anaheim."

The word *Enemy* is capitalized when referring to Satan (as is the Devil, the Evil One, and Father of Lies), but lowercased when referring to satanic forces.

The word *garden* is lowercased when referring to Eden or Gethsemane, whether or not those names are mentioned.

The word *gospel* is lowercased, except when referring to the Gospels (all of the first four books of the New Testament as a group). Do not capitalize when referring to a single book ("the *gospel* of Mark").

The words *heaven* and *hell* are lowercased.

The word *kingdom* is lowercased, even when referring to God's kingdom or the kingdom of heaven.

God's Word is capitalized when referring to the Bible; *God's word* is lowercased when referring to His statements or promises.

For Articles

The AP stylebook follows most of CWMS's rules for capitalization of religious terms. Some notable differences are:

Capitalize the names of major events in the life of Christ (e.g., the Crucifixion) unless the reference includes His name (Jesus' resurrection; the ascension of Jesus). Same for His mother (e.g., Immaculate Conception).

Capitalize *gospel* when referring to one of the first four books of the New Testament (e.g., the *Gospel* of Mark).

Titles and Headings
CMOS #8.155–8.158 and CWMS p. 106

When titles (and subtitles) of books, chapters, songs, poems, etc. and headings (and subheadings) are mentioned in text or cited in notes, capitalize the following:

> the first and last words of the title

> the first word following a colon or a dash

> all nouns, pronouns, verbs, adjectives, and adverbs

> conjunctions (*when, if, so, that*)

Lowercase the following:

> articles (*a, an, the*)

> prepositions (*about, down, in, on, over, through, up*)

> coordinate conjunctions (*and, but, or, nor, for*)

> the words *to* and *as*

Examples:

> Four Theories concerning the Gospel according to Matthew

> Looking Up Directions, Writing Them Down, and Typing Them Out
> (Note: *Up, down,* and *out* are used as adverbs here, not prepositions)

> Texting on Your Cell Phone in a Writers' Conference Workshop

---

For Articles

For titles of books, computer games, movies, operas, plays, poems, songs, TV programs, lectures, speeches, and works of art, capitalize:

first and last words of the title

nouns, pronouns, verbs, adjective, and adverbs

prepositions and conjunctions of four or more letters

Also capitalize the word *to* when it is used as part of an infinitive verb (as in, "Babette Smith To Publish Her First Literary Novel").

Note, *to* is not capitalized in article headlines, where only the first word, proper nouns, and the first word following a colon are capitalized.

Hyphenated Compounds in Titles
CMOS #8.159 and CWMS p. 45

When a hyphenated compound appears in a title, CMOS recommends the following guidelines:

- Always capitalize the first word in the compound.

- Capitalize all other words except articles (*a, an, the*), prepositions (*in, on, over, up, down, through*), or coordinating conjunctions (*and, but, or, nor, for*). Example:

Hard-and-Fast Rules for Writers

- If the first part of the word is a prefix that could not stand alone (*anti, pre,* etc.), lowercase the second part of the word (unless it's a proper name). Example:

  A Non-Christian's Guide to Post-resurrection Philosophies

- In a change from the 15th edition, CMOS-16 now recommends capitalizing the second part of a spelled-out number or fraction. Examples:

  Sue's Twenty-First Chapter

  A Two-Thirds Majority

Small Caps
CMOS #10.8 and CWMS pp. 41, 45–46, 55

Although earlier editions of *The Chicago Manual of Style* have recommended using small caps in certain instances, CMOS-16 recommends not using them at all.

A.M. and P.M.
CMOS #10.42

CMOS-14 (and the original CWMS) recommended using small caps with periods for A.M. and P.M. But CMOS-16 and the new CWMS recommend lowercase with periods (a.m. and p.m.).

B.C. and A.D.
CMOS #9.35, 10.39

CMOS-14 (and the original CWMS) recommended small caps with periods for B.C. and A.D. But CMOS-16 and the new CWMS recommend all caps without periods (BC and AD).

Note: AD is placed before the date; BC after. Examples:

3000 BC

AD 62

For Articles

Lowercase with periods for a.m. and p.m.

All caps with periods for A.D. and B.C.

Abbreviations for Scripture Translations

The original CWMS suggested using small caps for abbreviations of Scripture translations (KJV, NASB, etc.). The new version advocates full caps (NIV, NKJV).

ADD YOUR OWN

My Favorite Capitalization Rules

Reference Book   Rule or Page #   Rule

COLONS AND SEMICOLONS

Colons
CMOS #6.59 and CWMS pp. 148–149 and AP

A colon introduces something (or a series of things) that illustrates or amplifies what is written before the colon. Example:

> The panel consisted of three agents: Ned Aloof, Terry Friendly, and Mel Charming.

Capitalization with Colons
CMOS #6.61 and CWMS p. 148 and AP

The first word following a colon is lowercased unless (a) the first word after the colon is a proper noun, (b) the colon introduces two or more related sentences, (c) the colon announces a definition, or (d) the colon precedes a quotation or a speech in dialogue. Examples:

> Latisha had two choices: Should she try to write a steamy romance novel? Or go for a self-help book about punctuation addiction?

> Matthew 6:24 makes this clear: "You cannot serve both God and money."

> Kevin: My book has already been printed.
> Timothy: Then you can't correct the error until the second printing.

Semicolons in Compound Sentences
CMOS #6.54 and CWMS p. 370 and AP

A semicolon should be used between two parts of a compound sentence when they are *not* connected by a conjunction. Example:

> She removed the novel from the shelf; in its place she put a book on prayer.

If there *is* a conjunction, use a comma (unless one or both of the independent clauses contain a comma). Examples:

> She removed the novel from the shelf, and in its place she put a book on prayer.

> Sarah wanted to approach the Tyndale editor at lunch; but, since that table filled up before she arrived, she ended up sitting with the Multnomah editor.

Many publishers prefer that independent clauses be separated into individual sentences. Example:

> She removed the novel from the shelf. In its place she put a book on prayer.

Semicolons with *that is, for example, namely,* etc.
CMOS #6.43, 6.56 and CWMS p. 371

When expressions such as *that is* (*i.e.*), *for example* (*e.g.*), or *namely* introduce an independent clause, use a semicolon before and a comma after. Examples:

> Agents are essential for reaching the big commercial publishers; e.g., WaterBrook and Thomas Nelson.

To learn the appropriate punctuation rules, aspiring authors should study the industry-standard reference used by US book publishers; i.e., *The Chicago Manual of Style.*

Semicolons with Adverbs
CMOS #6.55 and CWMS p. 371 and AP

The words *then, however, thus, hence, indeed, accordingly, besides,* and *therefore* are adverbs; therefore, there should be a semicolon before them when they're used as transitions between parts of a compound sentence. (The preceding sentence is the example.)

ADD YOUR OWN

My Favorite Colon and Semicolon Rules

Reference Book	Rule or Page #	Rule

COMMAS

With Adjectives
CMOS #6.33 and CWMS p. 152 and AP

If a noun is preceded by two or more adjectives that could be joined by *and* without changing the meaning, the adjectives should be separated by a comma. Example:

> DiAnn proved to be a faithful, sincere friend.

If the noun and the adjective right before it are considered a unit, no comma should be used. Examples:

> Samantha has had many intriguing *romance novels* published.

> Jillian rejected traditional *royalty publishing* in favor of a small *subsidy publisher*.

With Adverbs
CMOS #6.25

Adverbs like *however, therefore,* and *indeed* are set off by commas unless the adverb is essential to the meaning of the clause, or if no pause is intended. Examples:

> If you don't enter the contest, however, you cannot win.

> If you write, you are therefore a writer.

> That was indeed what I did.

Cities and States
CMOS #6.46, 10.30 and AP

Always use a comma between city and state, whether the state is spelled out or abbreviated or designated by the two-letter postal abbreviation. Use a comma after the state except when followed by the zip code. Examples:

> Waukegan, Illinois, is not far from the Wisconsin border.

> Phoenix, Ariz., is my hometown.

> Fargo, N.D., is the location of my story.

> Send the proposal to 123 First Avenue NE, Fullerton, CA 92821.

Compound Predicates
CMOS #6.29 and CWMS p. 150

A comma should not be used between the parts of a compound predicate (two or more verbs having the same subject). Example:

> Kate took Evelyn to a writers' conference and talked her into signing up for two more.

Dates
CMOS #6.45

Dates in text include a comma only if the month and then the date precede the year. Example:

> On October 10, 1980, Donita submitted her fourth book in the series.

When using only the month and year (or date, then month, then year), do not use a comma. Examples:

> Copyright October 1980

> On 6 October 1924 Angelina wrote her first poem.

Dependent Clauses
CMOS #6.30–32 and CWMS p. 152 and AP

A dependent clause that is *restrictive* (that is, it cannot be omitted without changing the meaning of the sentence) should be followed by a comma when it comes before a main clause. Example:

> After she read Rene Gutteridge's book, Linda felt motivated to write a novel too.

A restrictive dependent clause should *not* be preceded by a comma if it *follows* a main clause. Example:

> Linda felt motivated to write a novel after she read Rene Gutteridge's book.

If the dependent clause is *nonrestrictive* (provides supplementary or parenthetical information not essential to the meaning of the sentence), it should be preceded by a comma.

> I'd like to borrow that book, if you don't mind.

> At last she arrived at the banquet, when the food was cold.

Phrases with Because

Sentences with *because* phrases can mean something dramatically different depending on whether or not a comma is used. Check out this example:

> Donald didn't submit a proposal, because he was afraid of rejection.

> Donald didn't submit a proposal because he was afraid of rejection.

In the first example, you're saying that Donald did not submit a proposal; after the comma, you explain why. In the second example, you're saying that Donald *did* submit a proposal ... but fear of rejection was not the reason.

Tip: Try inserting "Why?" in place of "because." If the sentence would make sense that way, use a comma.

Phrases with But *or* Yet

Sentences with *but* or *yet* phrases can present a similar problem. For example:

> I want to look as though my health has returned yet I am still in a fragile state.

> I want to look as though my health has returned, yet I am still in a fragile state.

Without the comma, you're saying this person wants to look healthy but also appear somewhat fragile. With the comma, you're saying she wants to give the appearance of being healthy, but she is actually still a bit fragile.

Note: If there's a possibility of misreading, move the dependent clause to the beginning of the sentence for clarity. For example, "Though I am still in a fragile state, I want to look as though my health has returned."

Phrases with Where

A comma before the word *where* can also change the meaning of a sentence. For example:

Sam walked into the classroom where he met Brooke.

Sam walked into the classroom, where he met Brooke.

In the first instance, you're identifying which classroom Sam walked into—the one where he met Brooke (presumably sometime in the past). In the second sentence, you're saying that Sam walked into the classroom, then you're telling what happened after he entered.

Phrases with Who

Same holds true for *who*.

After Jesus rose from the dead, He revealed Himself to two women who worshipped Him.

After Jesus rose from the dead, He revealed Himself to two women, who worshipped Him.

Without the comma, you're identifying the two women Jesus revealed Himself to, implying that they already worshipped Him. With the comma, you're indicating that these two women worshipped him *after* He rose and revealed Himself.

Direct Address
CMOS #6.38

A comma is used to set off names or words used in direct address. Examples:

> Mrs. Neumann, please come in.

> James, your order is ready.

> I am not here, my friends, to discuss my writing successes.

> Hello, Mrs. Philips.

A comma is used in salutations for informal correspondence ("Dear Sally,"); however, use a colon for formal or business correspondence, such as a query or cover letter ("Dear Mr. Laube:").

Exclamations
CMOS #6.37 and CWMS p. 153 and AP

Use a comma after exclamatory *oh* or *ah* if a slight pause is intended. Examples:

> "Oh, what a frightening cover," Lana shrieked when she saw John Olson's latest novel.

> "Ah, how charming," Paulette said when she finished the last book in Janice Thompson's first novel series.

No comma after vocative *O* or *Oh*. Examples:

> O mighty king!

Oh great warrior!

"Oh yes," "Oh yeah," and "Ah yes" are written without a comma. When spoken like a single word, "Yes sir" and "No ma'am" may be written without a comma. If "sir" is used in direct address, use the comma. Example:

No, sir, I disagree.

Independent Clauses
CMOS #6.28–6.29 and CWMS p. 152 and AP

An independent clause is a part of a sentence that could stand on its own as a complete sentence. If you put two of these together and join them with a conjunction (*and, but, or*), separate them with a comma. Examples:

Darlene looked startled by the acceptance, and Spencer nearly fainted on the couch.

Carl mailed the proposal, but he forgot to include a self-addressed envelope.

Exception: Short clauses don't need a comma. Example:

Heather designed the cover but Cheryl wrote the text.

Exception to the exception: Use the comma if there's a chance the meaning of the sentence could be misconstrued. Example:

Everyone was surprised by the arrival of the principal, and several students who had been gossiping in the hall rushed into the classroom.

Without the comma, someone might read, "Everyone was surprised by the arrival of the principal and several students ..." By the time the sentence is completed, the meaning is clear. But you don't want to make anyone go back and reread.

Interjections
CMOS #6.39

Commas should be used to set off interjections. Examples:

> Well, I don't like to brag, but my last book sold twenty copies.

> Well then, I guess I'll start a blog.

> Why, I can't even imagine that kind of success.

> Hey, I meant twenty thousand copies.

> Yes, I hired a professional editor.

> No, I didn't give up.

Introductory Phrases
CMOS #6.25, 6.35–6.36 and AP

An adverbial or participial phrase at the beginning of a sentence is followed by a comma. Examples:

> Blessed by the morning's devotional, Bethany sent an e-mail to the author.

> If your manuscript gets rejected, send it somewhere else.

Exception: A single word or very short phrase (fewer than five words) does not require a comma. However, if misreading is a possibility, or comprehension could be slowed, put the comma in. Example:

> In typesetting, the publisher can convert hyphens in numbers to en dashes.

You wouldn't want someone to read, "In typesetting the publisher, ..."

Use a comma after *now* (at the beginning of a sentence) when indicating a transition (e.g., "Now, this may not seem logical"). No comma when indicating the present time (e.g., "Now hear this").

Always use commas after prepositional phrases that could be removed from the statement without affecting the meaning: *for instance, for example (e.g.), that is (i.e.), namely, in any event, in the last analysis, as a result, in the long run,* etc.

Jr. and Sr.
CMOS #6.47 and CWMS p. 154 and AP

Jr. and *Sr.*, as well as numerals like *II* or *3rd,* following a person's name should not be separated with a comma. Examples:

> Harold Harrison Sr.

> Charles Winchester III

Participial Phrases
CMOS #5.109

A participial phrase (a participle plus any closely associated words) can be used as either an adjective or an adverb. The use of a comma depends on what the phrase is modifying. For example:

> Alice stood beside the cabinet holding her coat.

> Alice stood beside the cabinet, holding her coat.

Without the comma, the cabinet is holding Alice's coat. With the comma, Alice is holding her coat.

Here's another example:

> I found myself in the midst of an angry mob crying out for Jesus to be crucified.

> I found myself in the midst of an angry mob, crying out for Jesus to be crucified.

Without the comma, it's "the angry mob" that is crying out, and this person is standing in the midst of that crowd. With the comma, you're saying that "I" (the point-of-view character in this passage) cried out for Jesus to be crucified.

One more example:

> In the end, Jesus was left with 120 people cowering in an upper room.

If you put a comma after "120 people," you would be implying that Jesus was cowering in the upper room.

Restrictive and Nonrestrictive Appositives
CMOS #6.23 and CWMS p. 151 and AP

An "appositive" is a noun or noun phrase that immediately follows another noun or noun phrase in order to define or further identify it. An appositive that's "nonrestrictive" (restates a noun or pronoun in different words without changing or adding to the meaning of the sentence) is set off by commas. Example:

> My husband, Richard, got a promotion.

My husband's name is Richard, so either "my husband" or "Richard" could be eliminated from this sentence without changing its meaning.

If, however, the appositive has a "restrictive" function (it identifies the noun more specifically), it is not set off by commas. Example:

> My son Michael is eight years younger than his brother.

I have more than one son, which is obvious from the context of the sentence. "Michael" identifies which of my sons is being referred to in this sentence.

If you're not sure whether more than one thing exists, leave out the commas. Example:

> Carmen Leal's book *The Twenty-Third Psalm for Caregivers* is a tremendous blessing for anyone who is taking care of an ill or elderly relative.

However, in this case, you should do a little research and find out if the author has written more than one book.

If appropriate use of the comma could result in misreading or confusion, reword the sentence. For example, if you wrote, "My best friend, Chris, and I went to the book signing," a reader may wonder whether Chris is your best friend or if three people attended the event together. A better wording would be "I went to the book signing with my best friend, Chris."

Serial Commas
CMOS #6.18 and CWMS p. 151

In a series of three or more elements, separate the elements with commas. When a conjunction joins the last two elements in a series, use a comma before the conjunction. Example:

> Frank, Greg, and Ken discussed whether to give their wives copy paper, printing cartridges, or writers' conference tuition for their birthdays.

For Articles

The AP stylebook recommends leaving out the comma before *and* (or another conjunction) in a series, unless doing so would cause confusion or ambiguity.

Then and Too
CMOS Q&A, CWMS p. 154

The Chicago Manual of Style has an online Question-and-Answer section that addresses some issues not specified in the book. Here are two worth mentioning:

Use a comma before *then* when *and* or *but* is omitted but implied. Example:

> Susanne planned to publish novels in the CBA, then break into the ABA.

Use a comma with *too* only when you want to emphasize an abrupt change of thought. Examples:

There are several dictionaries out there, too, and they don't always agree on the spellings of all words.

Attending a writers' conference is a good way to learn novel writing too.

ADD YOUR OWN

My Favorite Comma Rules

Reference Book   Rule or Page #   Rule

DASHES

Two kinds of dashes are used in book manuscripts:

em dash —

en dash –

Tip: Some word processors can automatically convert hyphens to en dashes and em dashes. In Microsoft Word, go to Tools (or Word Options/Proofing), then AutoCorrect/AutoFormat. Put a checkmark in "Symbol characters/hyphens (--) with symbols/dash (—)." With this feature checked, follow these steps:

To make an en dash (–), type a letter or word, insert a space, then type a hyphen, then type the next letter or word, followed by a space.

To make an em dash (—), type a letter or word (do not insert a space), then type a double hyphen, then type the next letter or word followed by a space.

Alternatively, you can insert an en or em dash using "Insert/Symbols," then clicking on the "Special Characters" tab.

Another way to do it is to hold down the Ctrl key and hit the minus key on the numeric keypad for an en dash; for an em dash, hold down the Ctrl and Alt keys and hit the hyphen on the numeric keypad.

If you can't type dashes, CMOS #2.13 says that a hyphen may be used in place of an en dash, and a double hyphen can be typed to represent an em dash.

Note: *The Chicago Manual of Style* says there should be no space before or after either dash.

For Articles

The AP Stylebook says there *should* be a space before and a space after an em dash.

The en dash is not used in articles. (Use a hyphen instead.)

Note: *Web Style Guide* recommends not using en or em dashes for web writing since they are not supported in standard HTML text.

Em Dash

Use an em dash in the following circumstances.

Break in Thought
CMOS #6.84 and CWMS pp. 165–166 and AP

An em dash denotes a sudden break in thought that causes an abrupt change in sentence structure. Example:

Will he—can he—get the endorsements he needs?

An em dash is used in dialogue to indicate that one person's speech has been interrupted by another. If an em dash is used at the end of quoted material to indicate an interruption, do not insert a comma before the speaker attribution. (This is a change from CMOS-15.) Example:

"Honey," Mark began, "I was thinking—"

"About what?" Andrea interrupted.

"Well, I thought it could be helpful if I—" he mumbled, but she cut him off again.

For narrative that breaks up a line of dialogue, both em dashes go outside the quotation marks. Example:

"Someday I'll get published, but"—her voice cracked—"it won't be any time soon."

Complementary Element
CMOS #6.82 and CWMS pp. 165–166

A word or phrase that is added to or inserted into a sentence for purposes of defining, enumerating, amplifying, or explaining may be set off by em dashes. Examples:

Charlotte could forgive every insult but one—the snub by her coauthor.

Three novelists—Francine Rivers, Angela Hunt, and Karen Kingsbury—have most influenced my own writing.

Don't Get Carried Away
Dashes tend to stand out on a page. So if you have a lot of them in your manuscript, check each one and see if you could substitute commas or parentheses instead.

Never have more than one dash—or pair of dashes—in a sentence.

Never have more than one dash, or pair of dashes, in a sentence.

Never have more than one dash (or pair of dashes) in a sentence.

Here's another thought—try replacing a single dash with a colon.

Here's another thought: try replacing a single dash with a colon.

En Dash

In Numbers
CMOS #6.78 and CWMS p. 168

The en dash is used for connecting inclusive numbers, including dates, times, or reference numbers. It signifies "up to and including" or "through." Examples:

1981–1982

10:30–10:45

pp. 31–33

Daniel 13:3–15

Multiple-Word Compound Adjectives
CMOS #6.80 and CWMS p. 168

Use an en dash in a compound adjective when one of the parts is an open compound or when two or more parts are open or hyphenated compounds. Examples:

the post–World War II years

a hospital–nursing home connection

Universities
CMOS #6.81

Use an en dash to link a city to the name of a university that has multiple campuses. Example:

The University of California–Fullerton

ADD YOUR OWN

My Favorite Dash Rules

Reference Book   Rule or Page #   Rule

ELLIPSES

Fragmented Speech
CMOS #13.39 and CWMS p. 191 and AP

Use ellipsis points to indicate faltering or fragmented speech, often accompanied by confusion, insecurity, distress, or uncertainty. Examples:

> "I ... or rather, we ... yes, *we* made a terrible mistake," Emily cried.

> "These awful rejection letters ... what should I do about them?" Naomi moaned.

Ellipses are also used at the end of a line of dialogue when the speaker's words trail off. Example:

> "But Julie, I ..." Walter couldn't think of a valid excuse.

Like dashes, ellipses tend to stand out on a page. So use them as sparingly as you can.

Omissions
CMOS #13.48 and CWMS p. 192 and AP

Use ellipsis points to show that part of a sentence or passage has purposely been left out. This is often used when quoting Scripture. Examples:

Ephesians 3:20–21 says, "Now to him who is able to do immeasurably more than all we ask or imagine … be glory in the church … throughout all generations."

I am persuaded that neither death nor life … nor height nor depth … shall be able to separate us from the love of God. (Romans 8:38–39)

Quotations
CMOS #13.50 and CWMS p. 192 and AP

Ellipsis points should not be placed before or after a Scripture verse or other quoted passage (unless the quote is a sentence fragment or might be confusing to the reader), since it is assumed that the quote was taken out of a larger context.

Punctuation
CMOS #13.52 and CWMS p. 36

A comma, colon, semicolon, question mark, or exclamation point may be placed before or after the ellipsis if it helps clarify the meaning of the sentence. Examples:

For He spoke, … He commanded, and it stood fast (Psalm 33:9).

How long should a writer wait for a response to a proposal before contacting the publisher? three months … six months … a year …?

Ellipses with Periods
CMOS #13.51 and CWMS p. 192 and AP

A period is added before an ellipsis if the words that come before it constitute a grammatically complete sentence. When what follows the ellipsis is a grammatically complete sentence (even if part of the sentence has been omitted), the first word is capitalized. Example:

> Though I have all faith ... but have not love, I am nothing. ... Love never fails (1 Corinthians 13:2, 8).

Spacing
CMOS #13.48 and CWMS p. 193 and AP

In a manuscript that will be sent for professional typesetting, an ellipsis should be typed as three dots with a space between each (. . .). Put a space before and after an ellipsis used in the middle of a sentence. Example:

> "You can come in for a cup of coffee . . . if you take your shoes off first," Dana said.

During typesetting, ellipsis points will be separated from one another and from the text by "3-to-em spaces," also known as non-breaking microspaces.

If an ellipsis comes at the beginning or end of a quote, do not insert a space between the ellipsis and the quotation mark. Examples:

> "Well . . ."

> ". . . whether you like it or not."

If you prefer, you may use the single-character ellipsis created by most word processors when three periods are typed without spaces (...). If so, put a space before and after the ellipsis—except where it adjoins a quotation mark, parenthesis, or closing punctuation (as described above).

For Articles

Type an ellipsis as a three-letter word, with no spaces between the periods but a space before and after.

ADD YOUR OWN

My Favorite Ellipses Rules

Reference Book   Rule or Page #   Rule

_____

_____

_____

_____

_____

_____

_____

_____

_____

_____

_____

_____

_____

_____

_____

_____

_____

_____

ITALICS

For Articles

Italics are not used in journalistic-style articles.

Direct Thoughts

According to the 14th edition of CMOS (#10.43), unspoken thoughts, imagined dialogue, and other interior monologue, when expressed in first-person form, are typed in italics. Examples:

> Tracey looked at him in despair and thought, *Now what have I done?*

> Lucinda clearly heard God's direction. *Go apologize to Claudia. Now!*

The 15th edition of CMOS (#11.47), the 16th edition (#13.41), and CWMS p. 243 state that interior discourses *may* be enclosed in quotation marks or straight type, according to the writer's preference. Examples:

> "I don't care what he thinks," Veronica thought. "I'll never see him again."

> Lord, Sandra prayed, I wish I'd listened to You.

The reasoning behind this change is that long stretches of italics can be difficult to read and italics can be mistaken for emphasis. However, long sections of direct internal discourse should be used sparingly, regardless of how they're punctuated (with the exception of books that are written from first-person, present-tense point of view).

Italicizing direct internal discourse was the standard for a long time, and many publishers still use this format, though a few have changed to the new one.

Indirect Thoughts
CMOS #11.48

Interior thoughts that are indirect or paraphrased should not be in italics or quotation marks. Example:

> Melody told herself she didn't mind having to cut two thousand words from her manuscript.

Foreign Words
CMOS #7.49, 7.52 and CWMS pp. 242–243

Foreign words and phrases should be in italics if they will likely be unfamiliar to most readers. If a foreign word becomes familiar through repeated use in the manuscript, only italicize its first occurrence.

When foreign words become familiar through common use, they are often adopted into English. If Webster's Collegiate lists the word, don't italicize it.

For Articles

Foreign words that are not universally understood should be placed in quotation marks (with an explanation of the meaning in the text).

Letters as Letters
CMOS #7.59–7.60

Italicize individual letters of the alphabet unless used in a common expression. Examples:

the letter *s*

a capital *M*

He signed the paperwork with an *X*.

Mississippi is spelled with four *i*'s and four *s*'s.

But:

Mind your p's and q's.

Dot the i's and cross the t's.

My goddaughter knows her ABCs.

Letters used as school grades are not italicized.

Chloe got an A on her homework assignment.

Titles
CMOS #8.2 and CWMS pp. 244–245

Large published works that can be subdivided into smaller components (such as book titles—including subtitles—album titles, periodical names, movie titles, play titles, names of TV programs) should be italicized. Smaller, stand-alone components (chapter titles, song titles, section titles, short story titles, poem titles, titles of TV episodes) should be in quotation marks. The following paragraph contains several examples:

After watching the movie *Chicago,* Bill tried to read *The Hobbit,* but the tune to "All That Jazz" kept playing in his mind, so he decided to study a *Reader's Digest* article titled "Getting Stuck Tunes Out of Your Head."

CMOS #8.184 says that titles of *unpublished* works (theses, dissertations, manuscripts in collections, unpublished transcripts of speeches, and so on) are enclosed in quotation marks, not italicized. (The working title of a not-yet-published book that is under contract may be italicized.)

The title of a book series is neither italicized nor placed in quotation marks.

For Articles

Put composition titles (books, movies, plays, poems, songs, TV programs, lectures, speeches, and works of art) in quotation marks.

Exception: The Bible, and catalogs of reference materials (such as almanacs, dictionaries, encyclopedias, and handbooks), are not put in quotation marks.

Words as Words
CMOS #7.58 and CWMS p. 244 and AP

Italicize words used as words, or phrases used as phrases. Examples:

"The word *love* has many meanings, Amber," Antonio said.

"Is that why the phrase *I love you* is so hard for you to say?" she retorted.

Proper nouns used as words are not italicized. Example:

Always lowercase the first letter of the word *iPad*.

Quotation marks may be used in place of italics when italics are used elsewhere in the sentence, or when referring to spoken or quoted words/phrases. Examples:

The Spanish verbs *ser* and *estar* are both forms of "to be."

Many people say "I" when "me" would be correct.

Works of Art
CMOS #8.193

Titles of paintings, drawings, photographs, and other works of art are italicized.

Leonardo da Vinci's *The Last Supper*

Michelangelo's *David*

However, works of antiquity (whose creators are often unknown) are not italicized.

the Winged Victory

Venus de Milo

ADD YOUR OWN

My Favorite Italics Rules

Reference Book   Rule or Page #   Rule

LISTS

Vertical Lists after Complete Sentences
CMOS #6.124 and CWMS pp. 286–288

The best way to introduce a vertical list is with a complete sentence, followed by a colon. Items in the list have no closing punctuation unless they are complete sentences. If items run over one line, the subsequent lines are indented. Insert a blank line between the introductory sentence and the list. Below is an example.

> A book proposal should include the following:
>
> synopsis
> author bio and publishing credits
> market comparison
> title page with the byline centered under the title, and the author's name and contact information in the lower-left corner
> three sample chapters

Vertical Lists after Introductory Phrases
CMOS #6.125 and CWMS p. 288

If a list completes a sentence that begins with an introductory phrase, do not use a colon after the introductory phrase. Insert a blank line between the introductory phrase and the list. Put a comma at the end of each item. If any of the phrases in the list have internal punctuation, semicolons may be used at the end instead. Each item begins with a lowercase letter. A period follows the final item. Here is an example.

You can reduce redundancy in your writing by

avoiding repetition;
stating what you mean in the fewest words possible;
eliminating weak words like *actually, basically, definitely, extremely, so,* and *very*;
omitting unnecessary adverbs and adjectives.

Numbered Lists
CMOS #6.124–6.126 and CWMS p. 287

If the items in a list are numbered, a period follows each numeral and every item begins with a capital letter. Insert a blank line between the introductory phrase or sentence and the list. Items in the list have no closing punctuation unless they are complete sentences. Run-over lines are aligned with the first word following the numeral. This is an example.

Here are some of the most common mistakes beginning writers make:

1. Flowery writing
2. Overuse of adjectives and adverbs
3. Long sentences and paragraphs
4. Lack of transitions
5. Repetition/redundancy
6. Poor mechanics, including typos, errors in grammar and punctuation, misspelled words, and misused words

Bulleted Lists
CMOS #6.124 and CWMS p. 288

Bulleted lists follow the same format as numbered lists. Here is an example.

> To format your manuscript for a publisher, follow these guidelines:
>
> - Use wide margins, at least one inch.
> - Double-space all text. Indent new paragraphs five spaces. Do not leave extra space between paragraphs.
> - Use Courier or Times New Roman, 12-point font.
> - For special emphasis, use *italics*, not ALL CAPS or **bold**.
> - Never bind your pages in any way.

Note: Bullets are not recommended for web writing, per *Web Style Guide,* since they are not supported in standard HTML text.

For Articles

Use dashes in place of bullets for items in a list. Capitalize the first word following the dash. Use periods at the end of each section, whether it's a full sentence or a phrase. No space between the dash and the text. Here's an example.

> Jonas gave the following reasons for not trying to become a published author:
>
> —Never graduating from high school.
>
> —Failing ninth-grade English.
>
> —Fear of rejection.

ADD YOUR OWN

My Favorite List Rules

Reference Book   Rule or Page #   Rule

_____

_____

_____

_____

_____

_____

_____

_____

_____

_____

_____

_____

_____

_____

_____

_____

_____

_____

NUMBERS

For Articles

Spell out whole numbers below 10; use numerals for 10 and above. (This includes ordinals: *fourth; 21st.*)

Use numerals for ages of people and things.

Use numerals with million or billion in specific amounts ("The nation has 1.3 million citizens"), but use words with general amounts ("about a million dollars").

Use numerals for units of measure (speeds and weights).

Use numerals for fractions greater than 1 (e.g., 4 1/2).

Spell out fractions less than 1 (one-half, two-thirds, etc.).

Use numerals for temperatures (except zero).

Use numerals for all numbers in headlines.

Spell out numbers at the beginning of a sentence (except calendar years).

Numerals or Words
CMOS #9.2, 9.4–5, 9.7, 9.14 and CWMS p. 282

Spell out whole numbers one through one hundred, round numbers (hundreds, thousands, millions), numbers referring to someone's age, and any number beginning a sentence. Use numerals for all other numbers. Examples:

> We need fifty thousand copies of the book by May.

> If three more people sign up, I will need 121 copies of the handout.

> If I live to be a hundred and two years old, I will never understand punctuation rules.

> Nineteen eighty-seven was the year they met.

Below are some exceptions to that general rule.

1. Always use numerals with percents. Spell out *percent*, and don't use a hyphen. Example:

> Only 2 percent of the local population owns a Bible.

2. Use numerals for section and chapter numbers.

3. Use numerals in Scripture references.

> Paul talks about the armor of God in Ephesians 6:11–17.

4. Measurements (distance, length, area, height, etc.) are treated according to the general numbers rule. Example:

> Stanley is six feet one (or, more colloquially, six foot one).

Measurements with a combination of numbers and simple fractions may be spelled out if they're short, but better to write them with numerals. Example:

> I'm exactly 5 feet 4½ inches tall.

For Articles

Use numerals for measurements and spell out the words *inches, feet, yards,* etc. Hyphenate adjective phrases when followed by nouns. Examples:

> Larry is 6 feet 5 inches tall (but "the 5-foot-6-inch man")

> The basketball team signed a 7-footer

> The book is 6 inches wide, 9 inches tall and 2 inches thick

> The rug is 9 feet by 12 feet (but "the 9-by-12 rug")

In technical contexts, you may use the symbols for feet and inches—prime (') and double prime (")—with numerals. Do not use single and double quotation marks (' and "). No spaces between numerals and symbols. Example: 5'6"

Times of Day
CMOS #9.38 and CWMS p. 388

Spell out times of day in even, half, and quarter hours. Examples:

> seven o'clock

eleven thirty

quarter of four

five fifteen

Use numerals (with zeros for even hours) to emphasize an exact time. Examples:

The workshop starts promptly at 2:30 this afternoon.

If we leave now, we can catch the 6:20 train.

She woke up at five o'clock, but the meeting didn't start until half past seven, so she lounged around until six thirty, then missed her seven-thirty appointment.

For Articles

Use numerals for time of day except for noon and midnight (10:30 a.m., 5 o'clock). Spell out numbers less than 10 when used alone or in modifiers:

I'll be there in 15 minutes.

He scored with two seconds left.

A 12-hour day

The two-minute warning

Dates
CMOS #9.32 and AP

Except in dialogue, use numerals for dates (Example: December 4), even though it could be pronounced as an ordinal (December 4th).

When a day is mentioned without the month, the number is spelled out. Example:

> On November 5, Deirdre received her first book advance. By the seventeenth, she was lounging on the beach in Maui.

Consistency and Flexibility
CMOS #9.7 and CWMS p. 282

If several references to numbers appear in the same paragraph, you may treat them all alike to simplify the reader's comprehension. However, with similar items in a single sentence or paragraph, you may use both numerals and words. Examples:

> I've compiled a collection of short stories—one with 115 words, five with about 75 words each, and ten with only one or two paragraphs.

> Between 1,950 and 2,000 people attended the writers' conference.

For Articles

The AP stylebook says to stick to the basic number rules even in a series. Example: "The family had 10 dogs, six cats, and 14 hamsters."

Dialogue
CMOS #13.42

In fictional dialogue (and quotes from spoken sources such as interviews, speeches, movies, or plays), numbers that might otherwise have been written as numerals should be spelled out. Years are usually rendered as numerals, however, as are trade names that include numerals (e.g., 7-Eleven).

ADD YOUR OWN

My Favorite Numbers Rules

Reference Book   Rule or Page #   Rule

_____

_____

_____

_____

_____

_____

_____

_____

_____

_____

_____

_____

_____

_____

_____

_____

_____

_____

_____

PERIODS

Spacing between Sentences
CMOS #6.7 and CWMS p. 378 and AP

One space, not two, follows a period (or any other punctuation mark) that ends a sentence.

Abbreviations
CMOS #10.4, 5.220

Use periods with abbreviations that end in a lowercase letter.

e.g. ("for example")
(Only use this abbreviation within parentheses or in notes. And always follow it with a comma.)

et al. ("and others"—usually referring to people)
(*Et* is not an abbreviation, so no period there.)

etc. ("and other things"—never referring to people)
(Do not use "and etc." since *and* is part of the meaning. Do not use *etc.* at the end of a list that begins with *e.g.* or *for example.*)

i.e. ("that is")
(Only use this abbreviation within parentheses or in notes. And always follow it with a comma.)

Dr., Mrs., Ms., etc.

p. ("page")

pp. ("pages")

vol. (volume)

If the last word of a sentence ends with a period, don't add another period to close the sentence. You may, however, use other punctuation marks.

Genres include romance, science fiction, suspense, etc.

Do you think I could write romance, science fiction, suspense, etc.?

Do not use periods with abbreviations that are in all caps, even if lowercase letters appear within the abbreviation:

VP, CEO

MA, MD, PhD

UK, US

For abbreviations of states, CMOS recommends the two-letter postal codes (NY, IL, etc.); however, they allow for the use of state abbreviations with periods (N.Y. and Ill., for example). If periods are used with state abbreviations, use periods to abbreviate United States as well (U.S.). If periods are not used with state abbreviations, don't use them for United States either (US).

Note: According to CMOS 10.33, United States should be spelled out in running text when it's used as a noun. When used as an adjective, the abbreviation US is preferred.

For Articles

In text, use U.S., U.K., and U.N. (as both nouns and adjectives). In headlines, use US, UK, and UN (without periods).

Initials
CMOS #8.4 and CWMS p. 12

Initials standing for given names are followed by a period and a space. Examples:

J. R. R. Tolkien

C. S. Lewis

For Articles

Use periods but *no space* for initials in a name (to ensure that the first two initials don't get split onto two lines in typesetting).

Periods with Questions
CMOS 6.52, 6.68–6.69 and AP

Indirect questions get a period, not a question mark.

Yvonne wondered if she would ever get her memoir published.

Justin asked himself why he was afraid to approach an agent.

How to become a best-selling author was the question on everyone's mind.

When a question within a sentence consists of a single word (such as *who, when, how,* or *why*), a period should be used. The word may be italicized for clarity.

She asked herself why.

The question was no longer *how* but *when.*

A request, suggestion, or mild imperative ends with a period.

Could you kindly respond by March 1.

Would you please rise for the national anthem.

Can you shut the door.

Rhetorical questions often end with a period (or exclamation point), depending on the intended meaning.

Why don't we go.

How can you possibly think that!

Run-in Quotations
CMOS #13.66–13.67 and CWMS p. 137

After a run-in quotation (a quote that is included in the running text of a paragraph), cite the source after the closing quotation mark, followed by a period or question mark. Examples:

Jesus said to him, "I am the way, the truth, and the life" (John 14:6).

Was Paul advocating slavery when he wrote, "Slaves, obey your earthly masters in everything you do" (Colossians 3:22 NLT)?

If the quote is in the middle of a sentence, the reference is inserted immediately following the ending quotation mark, before any necessary punctuation. Example:

When Paul said, "Every knee shall bow to Me, and every tongue shall confess to God" (Romans 14:11), he was paraphrasing Isaiah 45:23.

When a quote comes at the end of a sentence, and it is a question or exclamation, that punctuation stays inside the quotation marks. Add a period after the closing parenthesis. Example:

When the Lord asked Cain where Abel was, Cain replied, "Am I my brother's keeper?" (Genesis 4:9).

Block Quotations
CMOS #13.68 and CWMS pp. 348–349

Cite the source of a block quotation in parentheses after the quotation (in the same-size type). Put the opening parenthesis *after* the final punctuation mark of the quote. No punctuation goes after the source. Example:

Then I saw a new heaven and a new earth, for the old heaven and the old earth had disappeared. And the sea was also gone. (Revelation 21:1 NLT)

Omission of Period

CMOS #6.14 and CWMS p. 220

No period goes after chapter titles, headings, subheads, etc. (unless they are immediately followed by text within the same paragraph).

ADD YOUR OWN

My Favorite Period Rules

Reference Book   Rule or Page #   Rule

_____

_____

_____

_____

_____

_____

_____

_____

_____

_____

_____

_____

_____

_____

_____

_____

_____

PARENTHESES

If an incomplete sentence is in parentheses, do not capitalize the first letter or add a period at the end. If the parenthetical comes at the end of a sentence, the punctuation goes after the closing parenthesis.

> I can't believe how much fun writing is (even though proofreading for punctuation drives me crazy).

You may include a question mark or exclamation point inside the parentheses if it goes with the phrase. Example:

> God loves us (mere mortals created from dirt!) with a deep, eternal love.

If what's in the parentheses is a complete sentence, it can be included as part of the sentence (middle or end). Do not capitalize the first word (unless it would be capitalized even if it didn't come at the beginning of a sentence). A question mark or exclamation point may be inside the parentheses if it goes with the parenthetical phrase, but do not put a period inside the parentheses.

> God cares about every detail of our lives (can we fully comprehend this?) because whatever concerns us is important to Him.

> Jesus existed from the beginning (He is eternal).

A complete sentence in parentheses can be punctuated as a separate sentence, starting with a capital letter and ending with appropriate punctuation inside the closing parenthesis.

Jesus' disciples physically handled God, the Word made flesh. (They walked with Him, heard His voice, and visibly saw Him.)

ADD YOUR OWN

My Favorite Parentheses Rules

Reference Book   Rule or Page #   Rule

_____

_____

_____

_____

_____

_____

_____

_____

_____

_____

_____

_____

_____

_____

_____

_____

_____

_____

QUOTATION MARKS

Double and Single Quotation Marks
CMOS #13.28 and CWMS p. 344 and AP

Use double quotation marks for short quotes within the text (run-in quotations).

> Jesus said, "Blessed are the poor in spirit" (Matthew 5:3).

Use single quotation marks for quotes inside quotes.

> "He said to them, 'Follow Me, and I will make you fishers of men'" (Matthew 4:19).

Note: In typesetting, the publisher will insert a "hair space" between a single quotation mark and a double quotation mark.

For Articles
Use single quotation marks for quotations in headlines. (Only in headlines, not in the text.)

Placement with Periods and Commas
CMOS #6.9, 6.50 and CWMS pp. 344–345 and AP

Closing quotation marks always come *after* a comma or period. Example:

> ACFW held workshops on "Characterization," "Point of View," and "Floating Body Parts."

Placement with Colons and Semicolons
CMOS #6.10 and CWMS pp. 344–345

Closing quotation marks always come *before* a colon or semicolon. Example:

> He wrote a poem called "When I First Saw Your Crooked Nose"; his girlfriend was unimpressed.

Placement with Question Marks and Exclamation Points
CMOS #6.10 and CWMS pp.344–345 and AP

Placement of question marks and exclamation points depends on whether the punctuation is part of the sentence as a whole or part of the quotation. Examples:

> Bob cried, "Did that acquisitions editor even read my proposal?"

> Jerry angrily replied, "He sure didn't read mine!"

> They have no basis on which to say, "We don't use this kind of material"!

> What gives them the right to claim, "Your work doesn't suit our needs"?

Block Indents
CMOS #2.18, 13.10, 13.20–13.22 and CWMS p. 345

Quotes of one hundred words or more (about six to eight lines of text), quotes of more than one paragraph, and quotes with lists should be set off as block quotations.

Block-indented quotes should be double-spaced (unless the rest of the manuscript is single-spaced), indented only on the left, with an extra blank line above and below the quote.

If the text following a block quotation is a continuation of the paragraph that introduces the quotation, it begins flush left. Otherwise, use paragraph indentation.

Block quotations do not begin or end with quotation marks. Only use quotation marks if they appear within the quoted text. Example:

> "As surely as I live," says the Lord, "every knee will bow before me; every tongue will acknowledge God." (Romans 14:11)

The first line of a block quotation should not have an additional paragraph indent. However, if the quotation consists of more than one paragraph, subsequent paragraphs should have the additional first-line paragraph indent.

ADD YOUR OWN

My Favorite Quotation Mark Rules

Reference Book   Rule or Page #   Rule

SLASHES

Abbreviations
CMOS #6.107

A slash may be used as shorthand for *per,* as in "90 miles/hour" or "$400/week," or in certain abbreviations, such as *c/o* for "in care of."

Alternatives
CMOS #6.104

A slash is commonly used to signify alternatives (an informal shorthand for *or*).

> he/she, his/her

> and/or

A slash is also used for alternative spellings or names.

> Hercules/Heracles

> Margaret/Meg/Maggie

Occasionally a slash can signify *and*—though still usually conveying a sense of alternatives.

> an editing/proofreading service

> an MD/PhD program

> a Jekyll/Hyde personality

Dates
CMOS #6.106

Slashes may be used in all-numeral dates (e.g., 3/10/12 and 9/11). Periods or hyphens are also acceptable (3.10.12 or 9-11). (Note: AP suggests using "9/11" for references to the attacks on September 11, 2001. No punctuation with "911" for the US emergency call number.)

Americans usually put the month first, but other countries do not. (Canadians and Europeans, for example, put the day first.) Therefore, to prevent ambiguity, dates should be spelled out in publications that may be read by people outside the US.

Fractions
CMOS #6.108, 12.45

Slashes are used to separate the numerator and denominator in fractions within the text (especially when the symbol isn't an option). Examples: 5/8, 3/16.

Poetry
CMOS #6.109, 13.27, 13.32–33

When two or more lines of poetry are quoted in running text, slashes (with a space on each side) are used to show line breaks.

If wishes were horses, / Beggars would ride.

A poetry quotation that runs longer than one stanza should be block indented, eliminating the need for slashes.

Spacing
CMOS #6.104

Where one (or both) of the terms separated by slashes is an open compound, a space before and after the slash can benefit ease of readability.

World War I / First World War

For Articles

The AP stylebook accepts the use of slashes in descriptive phrases such as 24/7 and 9/11, but otherwise confines its use to fractions and quoted poetry.

ADD YOUR OWN

My Favorite Slash Rules

Reference Book   Rule or Page #   Rule

GENERAL PUNCTUATION TIPS

Let me add two "rules of thumb" regarding punctuation.

1. Some punctuation should be used sparingly.

Avoid overusing exclamation marks. If your dialogue or narrative conveys the idea that a remark is shouted or a comment is extraordinary, you don't need to beat the reader over the head by adding an exclamation mark too.

Avoid long chunks of italicized internal monologue. (Avoid lots of short lines of italicized direct thought as well.)

Don't use too many semicolons. Most of the time, replacing a semicolon with either a period or a comma will make your text read more smoothly.

Don't overuse ellipses or dashes. A pause in speech may be indicated with narrative beats instead. Example:

"Stop." Zoe giggled. "That tickles."

2. When in doubt, look it up.

If you're uncertain about how to punctuate a sentence, get out your copy of *The Chicago Manual of Style* and take the time to look up the rule.

Don't drive yourself crazy doing this while you're writing your first draft (or even your second or third or fourth). But before you send your manuscript to an editor or publisher, make sure every comma, semicolon, colon, and dash is exactly where it should be.

Most writing techniques are subjective—once you learn them, it's up to you to determine how best to apply them to your work. But punctuation is objective. The rules are the rules, and you bend or break them at your own risk.

ADD YOUR OWN

My Favorite Punctuation Rules

<u>Reference Book</u>   <u>Rule or Page #</u>   <u>Rule</u>

_____

_____

_____

_____

_____

_____

_____

_____

_____

_____

_____

_____

_____

_____

_____

_____

_____

_____

_____

Section 3

Usage

Usage

Many words in the English language are spelled differently when used in different contexts, with different meanings, or as different parts of speech. Some words may be hyphenated, or spelled as two words, depending on how they're used in a sentence.

Unfortunately, even professionally published books sometimes contain usage errors. A writer friend of mine once noticed, on the back cover of a novel, a slogan that read something like "Christian fiction at it's best!" But "it's" is the abbreviation for "it is" or "it has." In this context, the word should have been spelled "its," without an apostrophe.

I often see billboards and advertisements, sponsored by big, well-known companies, advertising "low prices everyday!" But "everyday," when spelled as one word, is an *adjective,* which means it must modify a noun (as in "an everyday occurrence"). When referring to these low prices, the wording should have been "every day" (the adjective *every* modifying the noun *day*).

COMMONLY MISUSED WORDS

Here are the words I see misused most often in the manuscripts I edit (and sometimes in the published books I read). They're listed alphabetically to make them easy for you to find.

a while/awhile

a while (noun): a period of time

Jane spent *a while* editing her manuscript.

awhile (adverb): *for* a period of time

Mallory asked me to stay *awhile*.

accept/except

accept (always a verb): to receive, agree with, or say yes to

Bethany House did not *accept* Carol's proposal.

except (verb): to omit, exempt, or exclude

Luisa was *excepted* from the invitation list.

except (preposition): other than

Everyone *except* Nanette had the wrong answer.

Adrenalin/adrenaline

Adrenalin (proper noun; capitalized, without an *e* at the end): trademark for a product used in a preparation of levorotatory epinephrine

adrenaline (generic noun; lowercased, with an *e* at the end): a blood-pressure-raising hormone often used in nontechnical contexts

> A rush of *adrenaline* pumped through my body when I read that suspense novel.

advice/advise

advice (noun): a suggestion or recommendation

> Diana gave me excellent *advice* about publishing my book.

advise (verb): to suggest or recommend

> Ellen *advised* me to strengthen the conflict in my romance novel.

affect/effect

affect (always a verb, except for one use as a noun in psychology): to influence or cause a response

> This article will *affect* the reader's thinking.

affect (verb): to assume, to be given to, or to pretend

> Charmagne *affected* a silly manner of speaking.

effect (noun): result or accomplishment

What was the *effect* of this appeal for money?

effect (verb): to cause or bring about

The new manager will *effect* major changes in our sales methods.

effects (plural noun): goods or property

The deceased man's *effects* were willed to charity.

aid/aide

aid (verb): to provide something useful or necessary

One nurse can *aid* several patients during one shift.

aid (noun):

- a subsidy granted for a specific purpose ("financial *aid*")

- the act of helping, or help given ("providing *aid*," as in money or supplies)

- something by which assistance is given ("an *aid* to understanding")

aide (noun): a person who acts as an assistant

The *aide* helped the teacher hand out tests to the students.

aisle/isle

aisle (noun): passage

We met in the grocery store *aisle*.

isle (noun): island

We spent our honeymoon on a tropical *isle*.

all ready/already

all ready (adjective phrase): completely ready

The publishing house was *all ready* to offer me a book contract when my favorite acquisitions editor left the company.

already (adverb): previously

My book has *already* sold a thousand copies.

all together/altogether

all together (adverb phrase): in a group

Let's sing this *all together* now.

altogether (adverb): wholly, completely

The Lord is *altogether* holy.

allusion/illusion

allusion (noun): an indirect reference
Many passages in the Old Testament are *allusions* to the Trinity.

illusion (noun): a false impression

His affair shattered her *illusion* of a happy, healthy marriage.

altar/alter

altar (noun): a table or platform used in a church service

The new bride and groom prayed together at the *altar*.

alter (verb): to change

Roxanne hoped her outburst wouldn't *alter* their friendship in any way.

any more/anymore

any more (adjective phrase): any additional

"I don't want to hear *any more* backtalk from you!" Cissy hollered.

anymore (adverb): any longer

"I don't want to listen to you *anymore*," Randi cried.

back door/backdoor

back door (noun): a door in the back

Tony pounded on Jim's *back door*.

backdoor (adjective): indirect or devious

She suspected the men were involved in some kind of *backdoor* operation.

back-seat/backseat

back-seat (adjective)

Lance was a *back-seat* driver.

backseat (noun)

Ryan found a wad of gum on the *backseat*.

For Articles

Per *Webster's New World College Dictionary,* spell as two words (*back seat*) when used as a noun to mean "a secondary or inconspicuous position." Example: "Food takes a *back seat* to romance when you're in love."

---

back up/backup

back up (verb): to move into a position behind, or to make a copy of

"Don't *back up*," the waitress said, balancing the tray of food.

I *back up* my computer files every day.

backup (noun): a copy of computer data

I make a *backup* of my computer files every day.

backup (adjective): serving as a substitute or support

Wendy decided she needed a *backup* plan.

bad/badly

bad (adjective): suffering pain or distress

> I felt *bad* yesterday.
> (I experienced a condition that could be described as *suffering pain or distress.*)

bad (adjective): sorrowful or sorry

> Marion felt *bad* about mailing her manuscript.
> (*Sad* or *sorrowful* describes the *condition* she experienced.)

badly (adverb): in a bad manner

> Even minor errors reflect *badly* on publishers and authors alike.
> (*Badly* modifies the verb *reflect;* it describes *how* errors reflect.)

badly (adverb): to a great or intense degree

> If you want something *badly* enough, you'll work hard to get it.
> (*Badly* describes the verb *want*; it defines *how much* you want.)

CMOS #5.167 says that adverbs do not modify linking verbs (such as *appear, seem, become, look, smell, taste, hear,* and *feel*). When these verbs are used, the descriptive word applies to the subject, not the verb. (Example: He *seems* modest.)

To determine whether a verb is a linking verb, consider whether the descriptive word describes the action or condition, or the subject.

The sculptor feels *badly*.
(His ability to feel or touch is affected.)

The sculptor feels *bad*.
(He or she is unwell or experiencing guilt.)

best seller/best-selling

best seller (noun): a book that has sold more copies than most

best-selling (adjective): having sold more copies than most

Note: Never bestseller or best-seller

For Articles

Always hyphenate: *best-seller* and *best-selling*.

---

blond/blonde

blond (noun): a boy or man with blond hair

Sven, a muscular *blond*, strode the beach as if he owned it.

blond (adjective): of a golden, light auburn, or pale yellowish-brown color

Ted shook the water out of his thick mane of *blond* hair.

blond (adjective): having blond hair (when used of a boy or man)

Terrence was a *blond* man.

Blonde is the feminine version of *blond* for both noun and adjective.

Sasha loved being a platinum *blonde*.

Virginia dried her long *blonde* hair with a sandy beach towel.

For Articles

Use *blond* as a noun for males, *blonde* as a noun for females.

Use *blond* as an adjective for both males and females.

---

brake/break

brake (noun): the pedal that slows a vehicle

Hit the *brake* now!

brake (verb): to reduce speed

To *brake* the vehicle, press on the left pedal.

break (verb): to separate, fracture, or destroy

Why did I have to *break* my wrist now? I was planning to *break* up with my boyfriend tonight.

break (noun): condition produced by breaking, place where a break occurred, or interruption

The *break* in the storm gave Sharon a chance to walk outside for the first time since she suffered that ankle *break*.

breath/breathe

breath (always a noun): the inhalation or exhalation of air

Tamara's *breath* misted in the cold air.

breath (noun): a slight indication or suggestion

the faintest *breath* of a scandal.

breathe (always a verb): to inhale or exhale air

If you *breathe* deeply you will feel better.

breathe (verb): to feel free of restraint

Martha needed room to *breathe*.

breathe (verb): to permit the passage of air

This fabric really *breathes*.

breathe (verb): to utter or express

"Don't *breathe* a word," Nick begged.

callous/callus

callous or ***calloused*** (adjective): having calluses, or feeling no emotion or sympathy

The suspect's *calloused* hands revealed an occupation involving physical labor.

The reporter was a cold, *callous* man.

callous (verb): to make callous

> A childhood of abuse can *callous* a person to the needs of others.

callus (noun): a hard, thickened area on skin or bark

> The *calluses* on his hands reminded Shannon of a farmer she once dated.

callus (verb): to cause calluses to form

> The physical labor *callused* his fingertips and palms.

Note: *Mucous/mucus* follows the same rule.

capital/capitol

capital (noun): money or possessions; a column; a city serving as a seat of government

> I leaned against the *capital* outside the bank, thinking about making a *capital* investment before moving to the *capital* of Iowa.

capital (adjective): punishable by death

> Murder is a *capital* offense.

capital (adjective): chief in importance or influence

> Professional editing is of *capital* importance.

capital (adjective): excellent

That was a *capital* book.

capital (adjective): not lowercased

That word is spelled with a *capital M*.

A *capitol* is a building, or group of buildings, where government functions are carried out. When capitalized, it refers to the building where Congress meets in Washington. "*Capitol* Hill" refers to the legislative branch of the US government.

car pool/carpool

car pool (noun): an arrangement in which a group of people commute together by car, or the group entering into such an arrangement

carpool (verb): to participate in a car pool

cite/sight/site

cite (verb): to recall, remind, mention, or specify

Vie *cited* Ephesians 2:10 as her life verse.

sight (noun): eyesight, vision, or outlook

"Out of *sight*, out of mind," Kayla said.

The *sight* of Janet's face left him breathless.

sight (noun) can be negative, meaning eyesore, mess, or monstrosity.

> Rochelle's teenage daughter's room was a *sight*.

sight (noun) can also be positive.

> Tiffany was a *sight* for sore eyes.

site (noun): place, location, situation, scene, or locale

> The burial *site* was at Rose Hills Mortuary.

clench/clinch

clench (verb): to set or close tightly (Note: *Clench* is a "transitive verb," which means it requires an object, such as hands, fingers, jaws, or teeth.)

> Melissa *clenched* her teeth when Myra *clenched* her fist.

clinch (verb): to settle, to make final or irrefutable, or to secure conclusively (Note: *Clinch* is most often used for the securing of an agreement, argument, or verdict.)

> Jeanette's evidence *clinched* the argument.

clinch (verb): to hold an opponent in close quarters (a boxing term)

clinch (noun): an act or instance of clinching in boxing, or an embrace

coarse/course

coarse (adjective): not fine

coarse cloth

coarse language

course (noun): a path, customary procedure, or part of a meal

in due course

of course

three-course dinner

collision course

correspondence course

golf course

course (verb): to pursue or move swiftly

Airplanes coursed across the sky above her apartment every day, ruining the mood for writing romantic song lyrics.

Hot blood coursed through Brenda's veins as she wrote her suspense novel.

complement/compliment

complement (noun): something that completes

This book contains a full *complement* of screenwriting techniques.

complement (verb): to complete

That jewelry *complements* Kristen's dress.

The two coauthors *complement* each other with their different abilities.

compliment (noun): flattery or praise

Arlene enjoyed the *compliment* Elaine paid her.

complementary/complimentary

complementary (adjective): relating to one of a pair of contrasting items

Complementary colors appear directly across from each other on the color wheel.

complementary (adjective): mutually supplying each other's lack

Steak and seafood are *complementary* dishes for the menu.

complimentary (adjective): expressing or containing a compliment

Kathy Tyers's latest novel received many *complimentary* reviews.

complimentary (adjective): given as a courtesy or favor

A slice of pie is *complimentary* with your meal.

council/counsel

council (noun): an assembly/meeting or an advisory or legislative group

> city *council*

counsel (noun): advice, or a lawyer or consultant

> Anne gave me good *counsel* when she suggested I hire legal *counsel*.

counsel (verb): to advise or consult

> June's agent *counseled* her not to sign the book contract.

desert/dessert

desert (noun): an arid region (pronounced "DEH-zert")

> While roaming in the *desert*, Kelly lost her way.

deserts (noun): a deserved reward or punishment (pronounced "di-ZERTS")

> Danny got his just *deserts*.

desert (adjective): arid (pronounced "DEH-zert")

> Austin landed on a *desert* island.

deserted (adjective): uninhabited (pronounced "di-ZERT-ed")

Barbara landed on a *deserted* island.

desert (verb): to withdraw or leave, usually without the intent to return (pronounced "di-ZERT")

Do not *desert* me now.

dessert (noun): a sweet pastry, or the final course of a meal (pronounced "di-ZERT")

My grandmother always eats *dessert* first.

disc/disk

disc (noun): used for phonograph records and related terms

compact *disc* (CD)

digital video *disc* (DVD)

disc jockey

laser *disc*

disc brakes

disk (noun): used for computer-related references and medical references

solar *disk* (the seemingly flat figure of a celestial body)

slipped *disk* (round, flat anatomical structure)
a flower's *disk* (the central part of a flower head)

hard *disk* or floppy *disk* (round, flat plate coated with a magnetic substance on which computer data is stored)

discreet/discrete

discreet (adjective): prudent, cautious, careful, trustworthy, or circumspect

Never one to gossip, Rebecca kept a *discreet* silence.

discrete (adjective): separate, distinct, apart, or detached
This question consists of six *discrete* parts.

drunk/drunken

drunk (adjective): a current state of intoxication

a *drunk* driver

legally *drunk*

drunken (adjective): habitual intoxication or the behavior of intoxicated people

a *drunken* sot

a *drunken* brawl

For Articles

Use *drunk* after a form of the verb *to be*.

He was *drunk*.

Use *drunken* before nouns.

a *drunken* driver; *drunken* driving

---

elicit/illicit

elicit (verb): to draw forth or bring out; to call forth or draw out

> Poetry can *elicit* vivid memories and deep emotions in readers.

illicit (adjective): not permitted; unlawful

> I wrote that book without engaging in any *illicit* activities.

elusive/illusive

elusive (adjective): difficult to grasp, isolate, or identify

> Her novel contained so many *elusive* concepts I had difficulty following the plot.

> The *elusive* criminal led the search party farther into the woods.

illusive (adjective): based on or producing illusion; deceptive

> The murderer's *illusive* clues took the detective on several wild goose chases.

Memory Device: *Elusive* is the adjective form of the verb *elude* (meaning "avoid, escape"). *Illusive* is the adjective form of *illusion* (meaning "deceiving, misleading").

emigrate/immigrate

emigrate (verb): to leave a country to live somewhere else

immigrate (verb): to come into a country to live there

eminent/immanent/imminent

eminent (adjective): conspicuous, prominent

The old man had an *eminent* nose.

immanent (adjective): inherent

Writing success is 10 percent *immanent,* 90 percent learned through hard work.

imminent (adjective): ready to take place

Live as if the Lord's return is *imminent.*

ensure/insure

ensure (verb): to assure, to secure, to make something certain or sure

Jennifer wanted to *ensure* that her manuscript was received by the publisher.

insure (verb): to provide or obtain insurance on or for, or to contract to give or take insurance

Allstate *insured* the property against theft and vandalism, but not terrorism.

Note: Webster's Collegiate states that *ensure* and *insure* are somewhat interchangeable. However, *ensure* tends to imply a guarantee (as in, "His agent *ensured* the legality of the contract"), while *insure* stresses the taking of necessary measures beforehand ("Careful planning should *insure* the success of your book signing").

entitled/titled

entitled (verb): to give a title to, or to furnish with grounds for claiming

This ticket *entitles* the bearer to one free book.

titled (verb): to designate or call by a title

If you like writing church plays, you'll love my booklet *titled Christian Drama Publishing*.

Note: The Q&A section of CMOS Online says that *entitle* is "widely used, and many writers think it makes a better verb" than *title*. "The belief that *entitle* must not be used in place of *title* is one of many spurious 'zombie rules' clung to by writers and editors and teachers."

In my opinion, since many writers, editors, and teachers (and *Merriam-Webster's Collegiate Dictionary*) do not consider these words interchangeable, you're better off following the distinction to avoid having some of your readers think you're wrong.

every day/everyday

Every day is a combination of an adjective and a noun, synonymous with "each day."

Daisy wrote two thousand words *every day*.

Everyday is an adjective, which means it describes a noun.

For Josh, writing was an *everyday* activity.

face up/faceup

face up (verb): to confront or deal directly with someone or something

Writers need to *face up* to their fears.

faceup (adverb): with the face up

The peanut-butter toast landed *faceup* on the floor.

Note: ***Facedown*** (adverb) is one word.

The teenager slid *facedown* on the waterslide.

But ***face-first*** (adjective and adverb) is hyphenated.

Andi tripped and hit the wall *face-first*.

But ***headfirst*** (adjective and adverb) is not hyphenated.

The runner dove *headfirst* into home base.

farther/further

farther (adverb): at a greater distance (referring to a measurable length or space)

The ball traveled ten yards *farther*.

further (adverb): to a greater degree or extent

Brendon wanted to discuss the problem *further*.

fliers/flyers

fliers (noun): people who fly

flyers (noun): pieces of paper on which something is printed

Memory Device: *I* can fly on a plane; there's an *i* in *fliers*. *Flyers* only fly if you fold them into *y*-shaped paper airplanes.

For Articles

According to the AP stylebook and the dictionary they recommend, *fliers* is used to refer to both aviators and handbills. *Flyers* is only used when referring to certain trains and buses (for example, The Western Flyer).

---

foreword/forward

foreword (noun): a page or two of comments at the beginning of a book

forward (adverb, adjective): in front, or toward the front

forward (noun): a player on a sports team who tries to score points in a game

good/well

good (adjective): favorable, suitable, advantageous, agreeable a *good* time

a *good* book

good (adjective): free from infirmity or sorrow

I feel *good*.

He felt *good* about presenting his proposal at the conference.

In the above instances, *feel* is used as a "linking verb," which makes the word *good* the idiomatic equivalent of "in good health."

Good is sometimes used as an adverb in colloquial speech. (Examples: "You wrote that scene real *good*" or "I'm doing *good*, thanks.") This usage should not appear in narrative writing (except to portray a character's unique speaking style).

well (adjective): healthy

He's not a *well* man.

well (adverb): rightly, satisfactorily, expertly

That plot device works *well*.

Do not use *well* as an adverb with the linking verb *feel*, as "I feel well" would mean your sense of touch is working properly.

good night/good-night

good night (adjective/verb): used as a greeting or to describe a particular evening

"*Good night*, darling," Carolyn whispered after the door closed.

"Tuesday was a *good night* for him," Jay said, recalling how lucid his grandfather had been.

good-night (compound adjective): hyphenated only when followed by a noun

a *good-night* kiss

grown up/grown-up

grown up (verb phrase): having achieved adulthood

My last child is all *grown up* now.

grown-up (noun): an adult

We're all *grown-ups* here.

grown-up (adjective): like an adult

That's a very *grown-up* perspective.

home school/homeschool

home school (noun): a school taught in someone's home

All of Lynn's children graduated from *home school*.

homeschool (verb): to teach school at home

Alberta *homeschooled* her first child for two years; she *homeschools* the second one now; she plans on *homeschooling* the youngest one through high school.

Note: *Homeschooler* (noun) is one word. Example:

Steve found a support group for *homeschoolers*.

For Articles

The AP stylebook has:

home-school (verb)

home-schooler (noun)

home-schooled (adjective)

home schooling (noun—no hyphen)

---

in to/into

in to (*in* is an adverb; *to* is a preposition)

Judith turned her manuscript *in to* the publisher.

into (preposition) indicates movement or direction to an interior location, or a change of condition or form.

Sonja transformed her rough draft *into* a publishable manuscript.

Note: If you wrote, "As long as I turn my proposal *into* the right editor at the conference, I will definitely get published," you would be implying that you had plans to somehow put your proposal *inside* the editor (an interior location) or to make your proposal *become* an editor (a change of condition or form). In either case, you probably won't get published that way.

it's/its

it's is the contraction of "it is" or "it has."

> *It's* clear to me now how *it's* become such a common mistake.

its is possessive

> Wanda knew the manuscript had *its* faults, but she didn't know how to fix them.

Note: There is no such word as *its'*.

jeep/Jeep

jeep (noun): a military vehicle

Jeep (noun): a make of four-wheel-drive civilian vehicles

lead/led

lead (noun, long *e* sound): direction or example

> Follow my *lead*.

lead (noun, short *e* sound): a heavy, soft metal

led (past-tense verb): to show the way, or to conduct or escort

The experiment *led* Brock to believe that *lead* was the best material to use.

lightening/lightning

lightening (verb): becoming lighter; illuminating, shining, brightening; making something brighter; reducing in weight or quantity

> The acceptance from the publisher went a long way toward *lightening* Dalaina's mood.

> Sybil's boss refused to consider *lightening* her duties after the accident.

lightning (noun/adjective): the flash of light in the sky that usually accompanies thunder

> The *lightning* bolt lit up the night sky for an instant.

loose/lose

loose (adjective): not tightly bound (rhymes with "goose")

> Publishers prefer to receive *loose* pages rather than three-ring binders.

lose (verb): to suffer the loss of (rhymes with "ooze")

> "How did you *lose* so much money?" Crystal asked.

nauseated/nauseous

nauseated: feeling sickness, or being queasy

Dorothy became *nauseated.*

nauseous*:* causing sickness, or afflicted with nausea or disgust

The fumes were *nauseous.*

Note: Some people do not acknowledge the second meaning of the word *nauseous,* and if you wrote, "Rob is nauseous," they would understand you to be saying that he *causes* sickness. However, the most recent edition of Webster's Collegiate notes that *nauseous* is frequently used to mean "physically affected with nausea," usually after a linking verb such as *feel* or *become.*

For Articles

The AP stylebook does not accept the second meaning of *nauseous.* It says, "You feel *nauseated* (sick) from something *nauseous* (sickening)." Their dictionary says the second meaning is "rare."

---

on to/onto

on to (*on* is an adverb and *to* is a preposition)

We moved *on to* the next building.

On modifies the verb *moved*—"on" is how we moved. *To* is the beginning of the prepositional phrase "*to* the next building."

onto (preposition) means "to a position on." (Indicates that the subject is moving from one thing *to the top of* something else.)

He helped her step *onto* the high platform.

The dog jumped *onto* the table.

oral/verbal

oral (adjective): spoken

They observed several *oral* traditions.

oral (adjective): pertaining to the mouth

The doctor administered an *oral* vaccine.

verbal (adjective): relating to or consisting of words

The teacher gave the students *verbal* instructions.

verbal (adjective): spoken as opposed to written

We made a *verbal* contract.

passed/past

passed (verb): past tense of *pass*, meaning "to move or go away"

The car *passed* us at sixty miles an hour.
Uncle Vincent *passed* away ten years ago.

past (adjective): gone or elapsed

Your troubles are now *past*.

past (preposition): beyond

Jessica drove *past* the house.

past (noun): a time gone by

> Vickie regretted the *past*.

peak/peek/pique

peak (noun): top, apex, or summit

> JoAnn had reached the *peak* of her writing career.

peek (noun or verb): gander, glance, or glimpse

> She took a *peek* at Cal's manuscript after he *peeked* at hers.

pique (verb): to provoke, motivate, or stimulate

> The manuscript *piqued* the interest of several publishers.

pique (verb): to irritate, aggravate, or arouse anger or resentment

> Improper use of words really *piques* editors.

pique (noun): a transient feeling of wounded vanity

> In a fit of *pique,* she ripped the rejection letter into shreds.

peal/peel

peal (verb): to give forth loudly

> The church bells *pealed* at their wedding.

peel (verb): to strip off an outer layer

> Henry *peeled* an orange.

personal/personnel

personal (adjective): relating to a person, or done in person

This is a *personal* matter involving Judy and me.

He conducted a *personal* interview.

personnel (noun): a group of persons (usually employed at the same place)

The *personnel* in this office is very friendly.
(Note: A "group" is singular, so use the singular verb form.)

pore/pour

pore (verb): to read seriously and intently (usually used with *over*)

He found Daryl in the den, *poring* over the documents.

pour (verb): to cause to flow in a stream, or to dispense from a container

Denny *poured* the coffee.

pour (verb): to give full expression to

Jamie *poured* out her feelings.

pour (verb): to rain hard

It was *pouring* yesterday, but today is bright and sunny.

premier/premiere

premier (adjective): first in time (earliest), position, rank, or importance

Bonnie's *premier* performance was in community theater.

premiere (noun): a first performance or exhibition

The *premiere* of Abigail's play brought great reviews.

premiere (verb): to give a first public performance, or to appear for the first time as a star performer

Bernadette *premiered* in Hamlet.

principal/principle

principal (noun): a chief person

The *principal* of the school is a closet romance-novel reader.

principal (noun): a sum of money

Try to pay off the *principal* of your loan, not just the interest.

principal (adjective): main, foremost, first, dominant, or leading

His *principal* aim is to get published.

principle (always a noun): a guiding rule, a basic truth, or a doctrine

That statement expresses a *principle* of modern physics.

As a matter of *principle,* he refused to borrow money from anyone.

prophecy/prophesy

prophecy (noun): a prediction, foretelling, or revelation of things to come

The *prophecy* has yet to be fulfilled. (Pronounced "pra-fe-SEE.")

prophesy (verb): to predict, to foretell, or to indicate what is to come

What did the stranger *prophesy*? (Pronounced "pra-fe-SIGH.")

Memory Device: Pronounce the last syllable of the word *prophecy* and you will know it's spelled with a *c.* A prophet might "sigh" when he *prophesies.*

raise/rise

raise (noun): addition or increase

Aisha got a *raise* in her allowance.

raise (verb): to lift, uphold, resurrect, put up, build, or grow

Did Jesus really *raise* Lazarus from the dead?

Yvonne *raised* cherry tomatoes in her garden.

Note: The verb *raise* is always transitive (needs an object).

He *raised* his arm. (*Arm* is the object.)

rise (noun): an increase in amount, number, or volume

Crime is on the *rise* in Los Angeles.

rise (verb): to assume an upright or standing position

A gentleman should *rise* when a lady walks into the room.

Note: The verb *rise* is always intransitive.

The cream *rises*. (The cream isn't rising *something*.)

reign/rein

reign (verb): to possess or exercise sovereign power; to rule

The queen *reigned* over her royal subjects with a gentle hand.

rein (noun): a strap used to control an animal

rein (verb): to control, direct, check, or stop

Connor *reined* in his stallion a few feet from Angela's mare by pulling on the *reins*.

set up/setup

set up (verb): to cause, create, bring about; to put in a compromising or dangerous position; to begin business

Cathy *set up* shop just outside of town.

setup (noun): position, arrangement; something that has been constructed or contrived

It was a perfect *setup*.

some time/sometime/sometimes

some time (*some* is an adjective; *time* is a noun)

Christi and I spent *some time* together at the conference.

sometime (adverb): at some unspecified or unknown point in time (*at* is part of the definition)

I went to that restaurant *sometime* last year.

I'll do it *sometime* tomorrow.

sometime (adjective): occasional, or being such now and then

She was a *sometime* opera singer.

sometimes (adverb): occasionally
He visits me *sometimes*.

stationary/stationery

stationary (adjective): having a fixed or unmoving position, or not moving

This huge rock is *stationary*.

stationery (noun): writing paper and envelopes, or office supplies

This store's supply of *stationery* is almost exhausted.

Memory Device:
Stationary means "standing" or "staying." (Note the *a*'s.)
Stationery is used for writing letters with a pen or pencil. (Note the *e*'s.)

than/then

than (conjunction): used with comparative adjectives and adverbs

This book is older *than* I am.

That's easier said *than* done.

then (adverb): at that time; soon after; next

She lifted a heartfelt prayer, *then* put the proposal in the mailbox.

their/there/they're

their (adjective): belonging to them

Phoebe is *their* daughter.

there (adverb): in or at that place

I was *there* when it happened.

they're is a contraction of "they are."

We are disappointed because *they're* not going with us.

under way/underway

under way (adverb): in motion, or in progress

The flight will be *under way* as soon as possible.

underway (adjective): occurring while traveling or in motion

The fighter jet received an *underway* replenishment of fuel.

Note: It is usually preferable to replace "be under way" with *begin* or *start*.

The flight will *begin* as soon as possible.

For Articles

As of April 4, 2013, the AP stylebook suggests spelling this as one word, *underway,* as both an adjective and an adverb, although their dictionary only lists it as an adjective.

---

verses/versus

verses (plural noun): poems or passages of Scripture

versus (preposition): against, in contrast to

waist/waste

waist (noun): midsection

waste (noun): trash, garbage, something expendable

waste (verb): to squander

whiskey/whisky

Webster's Collegiate lists *whiskey* as the preferred spelling. But through a job I had in the beverage-services industry, I learned that if this liquor is made in the United States or Ireland, it's spelled with an *e*. If not, it's spelled without the *e*.

The AP stylebook says the spelling *whisky* is used only in conjunction with *Scotch*. However, their dictionary says US and Irish usage favors *whiskey,* while British and Canadian usage favors *whisky*.

weather/whether

weather (noun) refers to atmospheric conditions.

The *weather* will be sunny and mild.

whether (conjunction) is used with stated or implied alternatives.

It's true, *whether* you like it or not!

who's/whose

who's is a contraction for "who is" or "who has."

Who's going to write the next best seller?

Who's been using my manuscript as a coloring book?
whose (pronoun) is the possessive case of *who*.

Whose shoes are those?

whose (adjective): of or relating to whom

Carmen appealed to the editors, *whose* decisions were most important.

X-ray/x-ray/Xray

X-ray (noun): a radiation picture taken in a doctor's office (notice, capital *X* and hyphen)

The doctor took an *X-ray*.

x-ray (verb): to examine, treat, or photograph with X-rays (Notice, small *x* and a hyphen)

The doctor *x-rayed* Sherry's ankle.

Xray: communications code word for the letter *x*.

The policeman reported the license number as Alpha, Bravo, *Xray*.

For Articles

The AP stylebook has only one spelling for all forms of this word: *X-ray*.

---

your/you're

your (adjective): of or relating to you
Is this *your* blouse?

you're: contraction for "you are"

You're the best!

ADD YOUR OWN

My Favorite Confusing Words

Word	Part of Speech	Definition

Section 4

Grammar

Grammar

Entire books are written about all the facets of grammar, so I'll just touch on a few of the most common mistakes and problems I've come across in my editing.

COMMON GRAMMATICAL MISTAKES

among vs. between

In general, things are divided **between** two people or items, but **among** more than two. Thus, "The royalties will be divided equally *between* Heidi, Beth and Connie" implies that the money is to be split into *two* equal portions. Heidi gets half; Beth and Connie each receive a quarter. (The missing comma between Beth and Connie also supports the claim that Heidi gets half while Beth and Connie split the other half.)

Between can be used to indicate a one-to-one relationship when the number is unspecified ("cooperation between publishers"— could be two, could be more) or when more than two are specified ("between you, me, and the lamppost"). **Among** is appropriate when the emphasis is on distribution (such as dividing royalty payments) rather than individual relationships.

anxious vs. eager

Anxious indicates fear, nervousness, extreme uneasiness, or worry (*anxiety*).

Adriana was *anxious* about the exam.

Eager means enthusiastic, ready to begin.

Briana was *eager* to start writing her new novel.

as vs. like

Use **as** when comparing phrases and clauses that contain a verb.

Jeannie proofreads her work carefully *as* she should.

Use *like* to compare nouns and pronouns.

Chelsea writes *like* a pro.

both vs. both of

Use **both** (conjunction) when it's followed by two equivalent things. (See the comments on Parallel Construction later in this section.)

both this technique and that one

both my critique group and yours

Use **both** (adjective) when referring to a pair of things.

both novels

both book covers

Use **both** (plural pronoun) to refer to "one as well as the other."

Those are *both* good books.

Do you like fiction, nonfiction, or *both*?

Use **both of** before a plural object pronoun.

both of us/you/them/whom

Use **both of** before a noun phrase that starts with *the, these, those.*

both of the coauthors

both of those books

Use **both of** before *my, your, his/her, their* or the possessive form of a name.

both of my manuscripts

both of his novels

both of Isabella's publishers

both of Chicago's professional baseball teams

couple vs. couple of

Use *couple* alone when used as a noun.

Robert and Marcy made a cute *couple*.

When used as a modifier, add *of*.

It's never "a *couple* tomatoes." Always "a *couple of* tomatoes."

different from vs. different than

Things and people are *different from* each other.

"This guy is *different from* the other men I've met," Eileen said.

"Writing is *different from* speaking," Colleen said.

Different than is a convenient shortcut for "different from the way in which." In all but the most formal writing, than is preferable because it is shorter and tighter than "from the way in which."

Today's style of writing is *different than* it was in Benjamin Franklin's day.

For Articles

The AP stylebook does not recognize this "shortcut." For articles, always use the preposition *from*, never *than*.

---

each other vs. one another

Use **each other** when referring to two.

> Angie and Alan discussed the book with *each other*.

Use **one another** when referring to more than two.

> The critique group members discussed their manuscripts with *one another*.

fewer vs. less

Fewer refers to quantities/numbers.

> If you proofread your work carefully, you will get *fewer* rejections.

Less refers to amounts.

> First drafts require *less* work than rewrites.

> Note: One guideline is to use *less* with singular nouns (*less* money, *less* time) and *fewer* with plural nouns (*fewer* dollars, *fewer* hours).

filet vs. fillet

Filet mignon (noun) is a thick slice of beef cut from the narrow end of a beef tenderloin.

Fillet (noun) is a piece or slice of boneless meat or fish (including tenderloin).

Fillet (verb) means "to cut into fillets."

Only use *filet* with *mignon,* never by itself.

first vs. firstly (and other ordinals)

First (as well as other ordinals, such as *second, third, fourth,* etc.) can be used as an adjective (as in "The *first* book I read this year") or an adverb (as in "He *first* wrote a detailed outline and then typed the opening scene of his novel").

Firstly is an adverb, meaning "in the first place; first."

Since ordinals without the *-ly* can function as both adjectives and adverbs, *-ly* ordinals are considered superfluous by many readers. In addition, *-ly* ordinals can become troublesome when the numbers get above *fourthly* or *fifthly.*

Both forms are common in all types of writing. However, since some people consider the *-ly* ordinals wrong, or at least substandard, you will offend the sensibilities of fewer readers if you stick with ordinals that do not end in *-ly.*

hangar vs. hanger

Hangar (noun) is a covered and usually enclosed area for housing and repairing aircraft.

The plane is in the *hangar*.

Hanger (noun) is a device by which or to which something is hung or hangs.

Your favorite shirt is in the closet on a *hanger*.

if vs. in case

In verbal speech, people often use *if* when *in case* is grammatically correct. Consider this sentence:

> If you've never heard of Liz Curtis Higgs, she's an amazing author of both fiction and nonfiction.

Liz Curtis Higgs is an amazing author—whether or not you've heard of her. The goal of this sentence is to provide information *in case* the reader is unaware of it.

"In case" isn't the only way to reword an improper "if" statement. Take this example:

> If I can get an author photo on the back cover of my book, I'm attaching a couple for you to choose from.

You're attaching photos *in case* the publisher decides to use one for the cover. You could reword to something like this: "I would very much like to have my photo on the back cover. Attached are a couple of options you could choose from."

important vs. importantly

Important is an adjective.

Importantly is an adverb.

Webster's Collegiate gives two meanings for the adverb *importantly*:

1. In an important way

He contributed *importantly* to my career.

2. It is important that

More *importantly*, God's will is being done in His way and His timing.

Many people object to using *importantly* with meaning #2, preferring to use the adjective *important*. Webster's Collegiate says that both are acceptable. However, if you do use *important* in this way, it must always be preceded by *more* or *most*. Examples:

The book had plenty of mystery and suspense; *more important*, it had a strong Christian message.

The publisher offered several reasons for rejecting the manuscript, the *most important* being that the story has no main female character.

Importantly does not require *more* or *most*. Examples:

The book appeals to children, but just as *importantly*, parents will enjoy it.

Importantly, the story has a good balance of dialogue and narrative.

Since this is one of those things that some readers feel strongly about, my advice is to avoid using *importantly* for meaning #2, especially if it's preceded by *more* or *most*.

lay vs. lie

Lay and *lie* are arguably the most difficult irregular verbs in the English language. The main confusion lies in the fact that while present-tense *lie* and present-tense *lay* mean two different things, the past tense of *lie* is *lay*. In addition, when people speak, these words are frequently misused, so our ears are used to hearing them incorrectly.

Lay (present tense) means "to put or place something or someone down."

Lay is a "transitive verb," so it requires a direct object (the "something or someone").

Use present-tense *lay* when the action happens consistently or is happening presently.

We *lay* our lives on the line for Christ every day.

The past tense of *lay* is *laid.*

Ronit *laid* her five-hundred-page manuscript on the bed.

The past-participle form of *lay* is *had laid.*

Megan *had laid* the last page of her manuscript on the table seconds before her three-year-old spilled the two-liter bottle of soda.

Other examples:

> Carla *will lay* her notebook down only after she's written twenty pages.

> The dinner table *was laid* for six people.

> *Laying* tile is difficult work.

Lie (present tense) means "to rest or recline."

Lie is a state of being. It is an "intransitive verb," so no direct object follows. (Of course, there's another definition for *lie*, but it's not a problem word.)

Use present-tense *lie* when the action happens consistently or is happening presently.

> Candy's dog *lies* on the guest bed every night.
> (The dog is resting/reclining. No action.)

> Please *lie* down here.

The past tense of *lie* is *lay*.

> Ruth *lay* in bed all night, dreaming of the day her novel would be published.

The past-participle form of *lie* is *has lain*.

> Jill *has lain* in bed ever since her toddler spilled juice all over her manuscript.

Other examples:

The river *lies* between two hills; it has *lain* there for centuries.

The pen *is lying* on the desk.

literally

Literally (adverb) has two meanings:

1. In an actual sense or manner.

Reading horror novels *literally* makes my stomach churn.

2. In effect, or in a virtual manner.

My book will *literally* turn the publishing world upside down.

When I met him, my heart *literally* flew out of my chest.

Since meaning #2 is basically the opposite of meaning #1, many people consider it improper usage. In verbal speech, it often goes unnoticed. But in writing, it can be glaringly obvious. You don't, for example, want your readers to be pulled out of your story as they visualize the character's heart actually flying out of her chest.

Webster's Collegiate allows for *literally* to be used in a virtual sense, as hyperbole, to add emphasis. But in contexts where no additional emphasis is necessary or desired, it should not be used.

For Articles

The AP stylebook says *literally* always means "in an exact sense" and should not be use figuratively.

---

more than vs. over

More than is used with figures.

> *More than* one thousand people bought Tim's book.

> My romance novel has sold *more than* fifty thousand copies to date.

Over refers to spatial relationships.

> The football soared *over* the receiver's head.

Over can also be used with amounts. Examples:

> I paid *over* five dollars for that book.
> (One could argue that the number of dollars you spent was *more than* five; however, here "five dollars" represents an *amount* of money.)

> I spent *over* twenty years working on my first book.
> (One could argue that the number of years you spent was *more than* twenty; however, here "twenty years" represents an *amount* of time.)

myriad

myriad (adjective): innumerable

> Louise gazed at the *myriad* stars in the sky.

myriad (noun): a great number, or ten thousand

> They encountered *a myriad of* problems in their marriage.

She experienced *myriads* of difficulties getting her book published.

Note: Webster's Collegiate claims that the noun usage of this word is acceptable. However, since *myriad* has traditionally been used exclusively as an adjective, some readers find this use objectionable. (Consider replacing the singular noun *myriad* with *plethora*.)

For Articles

The AP stylebook has *myriad* only as an adjective, not as a noun (so never preceded by *a* and followed by *of*), even though their dictionary lists both uses.

---

reason, why, and because

reason (noun): explanation, justification, motive, or cause

why (noun, adverb, or conjunction): cause, reason, or purpose

because (conjunction): for the reason that

Here are some correct examples:

The *reason* Melanie writes fiction is *that* she loves reading it.

I don't understand *why* more people don't read novellas.

George writes nonfiction *because* he believes it helps people.

The following are incorrect:

> The *reason* Gwen writes fiction is *because* she loves reading it.
> (Here you'd be saying that the *reason* is *for the reason*.)

> I don't understand the *reason why* more people don't read novellas.
> (You're saying you don't understand the *cause cause*.)

> The *reason why* Todd writes nonfiction is *because* he believes it helps people.
> (Yikes! Here you're saying that the *cause cause* is *because*.)

that

CMOS #6.22 says that the pronoun *that* may be omitted if the sentence is just as clear without it. For example:

> The book (*that*) I just finished reading was amazing.

But don't go overboard with deleting every *that* in your manuscript. If it helps with flow and/or clarity, leave it in. For example:

> Jeff suggested the plan to make the main character a dragon was ridiculous.

At first read, it sounds like Jeff suggested this plan. By the end of the sentence, you realize that he said the plan was ridiculous. By putting *that* after *suggested,* this temporary confusion is eliminated.

Jeff suggested *that* the plan to make the main character a dragon was ridiculous.

Another note on this word. If you have *that* before a conjunction phrase or prepositional phrase, don't have *that* after the clause as well. For example:

What I meant was *that* when you get your first book published *that* I would have a book-signing party for you.
(Take out the second *that*.)

that vs. which

That is used with "restrictive clauses," phrases that narrow a category or identify a particular item in that category.

Manuscripts *that* are not solicited by the publisher will be returned to sender.

In this example, the category is *manuscripts*. The "not solicited" phrase narrows the category to *unsolicited manuscripts*. If you took out the phrase, you'd have "Manuscripts will be returned to sender," which would be different.

Which is used with "nonrestrictive clauses," phrases that add something about an item already identified.

My manuscript, *which* was not solicited by the publisher, was returned to me.

The item—"my manuscript"—is already identified. The "not solicited" phrase adds additional information. You could take out the phrase without changing the meaning of the sentence. "My manuscript was returned to me."

Note: *Which* clauses require commas; *that* clauses do not use commas.

that vs. who

That refers to animals and things.

The dog *that* bit me chased the Frisbee *that* I threw.

Who refers to people.

The man *who* bought Tammy flowers was handsome.

try and vs. try to

Try and should only be used when the subject is trying *and* doing something else.

Three times Dawn *tried and* failed to get her manuscript published.

Try to should always be used when referring to something the subject tried *to* accomplish.

Ariana is going to *try to* write her first draft in a week.

unique

Webster's Collegiate gives three definitions for this adjective:

1. Being the only one

2. Being without a like or equal

3. Unusual

The first definition dates back to the seventeenth century, but popular use of the word with modifiers (*somewhat, very, more, fairly, relatively, kind of,* etc.) resulted in the third definition.

However, people who don't accept (or know about) the recently added definition will object to using modifiers with *unique,* asserting that a thing is either unique (one of a kind, without equal) or it isn't. If you wish to avoid irking a percentage of your readers, you would be wise to avoid tacking adverbs onto this word. There are numerous synonyms you can use (*unusual, strange, peculiar,* etc.) that could be preceded by modifiers without bothering anyone.

was vs. were

Besides the obvious use of *was* as singular past tense ("I was there") and *were* as plural past tense ("We were there") for simple declarative statements, the subjunctive mood (*were*) is used to express the following:

1. A condition contrary to fact

   I wish I *were* a best-selling author.

2. A speculation

   Suppose Jack *were* to arrive right now.

3. An improbable condition

   Carrie drank the Pepsi as if there *were* no tomorrow. (Highly unlikely)

4. Uncertainty or doubt

> "If I *were* to marry you, how would you support me?" Irene asked.
>
> (There's uncertainty/doubt about whether she will marry him.)

5. Necessity

> "If it *were* absolutely essential, I could rewrite my manuscript," David said.

6. A desire

> Joan wishes she *were* going to the prom with Brandon.

Although the subjunctive mood is often signified by *if*, not every *if* requires a subjunctive verb. If the statement might be true but the writer doesn't know for sure, the indicative is called for. (See CMOS #5.121.)

> If Napoleon *was* in fact poisoned with arsenic, historians will need to reevaluate his associates.

ADD YOUR OWN

My Favorite Commonly Misused Words

Word	Definition	Confusion

MODIFIERS

Dangling Modifiers
CMOS #5.112

When you start a sentence with a modifying word or phrase, the subject of the sentence is what must be modified by that word or phrase. A "dangling modifier" is a phrase that does not clearly and sensibly modify the appropriate word. Example:

> *Changing the oil every three thousand miles,* <u>the Mustang</u> seemed to run better.

A Mustang cannot change its own oil. So you'd want to rewrite that as something like "By changing the oil every three thousand miles, Fred found that his Mustang ran better."

Another example:

> *Walking to work,* <u>the eucalyptus trees</u> reminded Nicole of a scene from a Brandilyn Collins novel.

Eucalyptus trees don't walk to work...not even in Brandilyn's novels. So rewrite: "As Hope walked to work, the eucalyptus trees reminded her of a scene from *Eyes of Elisha.*"

Example #3:

> *After forty days of fasting in the wilderness,* <u>Satan</u> tempted Jesus.

Satan didn't fast in the wilderness for forty days. So reword to "Following forty days of fasting in the wilderness, Jesus was tempted by Satan," or, "After Jesus fasted in the wilderness for forty days, Satan tempted Him."

Here's another example:

> *As a writer,* <u>words and punctuation marks</u> are the tools of your trade.

"Words and punctuation marks" are not "a writer." So rewrite to something like this: "Words and punctuation marks are a writer's tools of the trade."

And one more:

> *Six months after attending Mount Hermon,* <u>Kim's article</u> was accepted by a publisher.

"Kim's article" did not attend Mount Hermon. So rewrite to something like "Six months after Kim attended Mount Hermon, her article was accepted by a publisher."

Misplaced Modifiers

The position of a modifier determines what thing or action is being modified. Example:

> Mona sent out a proposal for her book on living with horses last week.

Mona's proposal wasn't for a book about "living with horses last week." Reword to:

Last week Mona sent out a proposal for her book on living with horses.

Example #2:

The editor told me on Thursday I have a book signing.

Did the editor say this on Thursday, or do you have a book signing on Thursday? Either of the following would be better:

On Thursday, the editor told me I have a book signing.

The editor told me I have a book signing on Thursday.

Simultaneous Modifiers

Be sure the introductory phrase can be accomplished *at the same time as* the action in the rest of the sentence.

Hugging the postman, Delilah ripped open the box containing her new novel.

Delilah cannot simultaneously hug the postman and rip open a box. Reword to:

After hugging the postman, Delilah ripped open the box containing her new novel.

ADD YOUR OWN

Incorrect Modifiers I've Caught in My Own (or Other Authors') Writing

Phrase	Subject of Sentence	Suggested Rewrite

PARALLEL CONSTRUCTIONS

CMOS 5.214 deals with what they call "paired joining terms and parallel structure."

Pairs of related conjunctions, such as *both–and, either–or, neither–nor*, and *not only–but also* (and some adverb pairs, such as *as–so, if–then*, and *where–there*), must be followed by grammatically parallel sentence elements.

both–and

The word *both* must be immediately followed by two grammatically equivalent options, with an *and* between them. Consider this sentence: "She shared *both* her most cherished and painful memories."

This is incorrect because the two phrases after *both* are (1) "her most cherished" (three modifiers) and (2) "painful memories" (adjective and noun). You could simply take out the word *both*. Or reword to "She shared *both* her most cherished memories and her most painful ones." Or "She shared *both* cherished and painful memories" (since the two things after *both* are "cherished" and "painful," which are adjectives).

Tip: Whenever you see *both* in a sentence, mentally add "#1" after the word *both* and "#2" after the word *and*, and see if the two phrases are equivalent.

either–or

The word *either* must be immediately followed by two options, with an *or* between them. The options need to be grammatically equivalent (two nouns, two verb phrases, two complete sentences, etc.). Consider this sentence: "If proofreading carefully is the key to becoming a best-selling author, I'm *either* not doing it right *or* I'm missing something."

This is incorrect because the two options presented are (1) "not doing it right" (verb phrase) or (2) "I'm missing something" (complete sentence). The word *either* has to come before "I'm not doing it right" (with the second option being "I'm missing something"—both complete sentences). Or you could take out *I'm* in the second option (so the choices become "not doing it right" or "missing something," both verb phrases).

Tip: Whenever you see *either* in a sentence, mentally add "#1" after the word *either* and "#2" after the word *or*, and see if the two options are equivalent.

ADD YOUR OWN

**Parallel Construction Issues I've Caught in My Own
(or Other Authors') Writing**

Phrase	Subject of Sentence	Suggested Rewrite

PRONOUNS

Pronouns as Subjects or Objects

I, he/she, we, they, and *who* are subject pronouns. A subject is the one initiating something.

>*I* like mystery novels.

>*He* writes best sellers.

>*She* listens to opera.

>*We* read nonfiction books.

>*They* are multi-published authors.

>*Who* reads historical romance?

Me, him/her, us, them, and *whom* are object pronouns. An object is the recipient of something.

>Luke was talking to *me.*

>Constance loves *him.*

>Jason likes *her.*

>Dad is taking *us* out to dinner.

>Please introduce me to *them.*

>To *whom* are you speaking?

Sounds easy, right? But it can get tricky when you have multiple people. For example, "Jeremy took Christine and I out to dinner" sounds right, but it's not. *I* is a subject pronoun, not an object. So "Jeremy took Christine and me out to dinner" is correct.

How can you be sure? Take out the other person. You wouldn't say, "Jeremy took I out to dinner."

The other time this is confusing is when the pronoun appears at the end of a sentence. Is it "Joel writes better than *me*" or "Joel writes better than *I*"? The trick here is to finish the thought. "Joel writes better than *I do*."

How about this one?

> Becky likes romance novels more than *me*.
> or
> Becky likes romance novels more than *I*.

Which pronoun you use depends on what you're trying to communicate here. Does Becky like romance novels more than she likes me? Or does Becky like romance novels more than I do?

When someone calls and asks to speak to Melinda, and you're Melinda, do you say, "This is her" or "This is she"?

The grammatically correct form is "This is she (who is speaking)."

Sounds pretty awkward, though, huh? You'd probably rather say, "This is Melinda."

The pronouns *who* and *whom* can be confusing. But there are some tricks you can use with these too.

1. Try substituting a he/she or him/her pronoun. If he/she fits, use *who*. If him/her fits, use *whom*.

Marty, *who* rented the room, left the window open.
(*He* rented the room.)

Marty, to *whom* the room was rented, left the window open.
(It was rented to *him*.)

2. *Whom* is always preceded by a preposition because the action has to happen *to, with,* or *for* the person being referred to.

The man *to whom* you wrote the check no longer works at this company.

The bowlers *with whom* I play won every tournament last season.

The audience *for whom* the book was written is teenage girls.

Pronoun/Antecedent Agreement
CMOS #5.28, 5.33

The *antecedent* is the noun to which a pronoun refers. The antecedent may appear in the same sentence as the pronoun or in an earlier one; occasionally, it comes after.

Here are some pronoun-antecedent rules to watch for in your writing.

1. Make sure every pronoun you use has an antecedent.

Amanda said she was going to the store.
(*She* refers to *Amanda*.)

Exception: The pronouns *it* and *who* can sometimes stand alone.

It's a beautiful day.

It's going to rain.

Who was at the door?

However, avoid using *it* when the antecedent could be confusing. For example, don't just write, "In Romans 3, it says ..."

Instead, write, "Romans 3 says ..." Or "In the Bible, Romans 3 says ..." (although that introductory phrase isn't necessary unless you think your readers might not know that Romans is in the Bible).

2. Don't start a new chapter or section with a pronoun.

If you open with "He pulled out a gun and aimed it at her head," your reader will have no idea who these characters are.

Chapter and section breaks often indicate a change in time, place, and/or point of view, so your reader cannot assume that the people referred to in the new chapter/section are the same ones talked about in the last one.

Note: If you're writing a suspense novel, you may want to keep the identity of a character a mystery. This is tricky, but can be done if you know what you're doing. Even so, it is better to use "the man" (or better yet, something more descriptive like "the skittish foreigner") instead of "he" at the beginning of a chapter or new section.

3. Don't confuse readers with unclear or ambiguous references.

Consider the ambiguity in following sentence:

> When Lori and Jan entered the room, Maddison noticed her right away.
> (Which woman did Maddison notice?)

4. Avoid using the word *it* in confusing contexts.

As Allison drove her car up to the service window, *it* made a rattling sound.

Does *it* refer to the car or the window? Rewrite to something like "As Allison drove up to the service window, her car made a rattling sound."

Audrey reached for her glass and drank it in one gulp.

In this sentence, the *it* refers to the glass, and she didn't drink *the glass* in one gulp.

5. Make the pronoun and its antecedent agree in number.

Trevor's two sons are sloppy. (plural)

Neither *one of them* combs *his* hair. (singular)

Portia's two daughters are neat; *they* both clean up after *themselves*. (plural)

Note: In an effort to avoid gender bias (using *he* to refer to both sexes) and the annoying repetition of *him/her, he or she,* and the like, some people use *they* as a singular pronoun when referring to someone whose gender is unknown or irrelevant. For example:

A writer (singular) needs thick skin if they (plural) want to work with a professional editor (singular) on their (plural) manuscript (singular).
(Makes me cringe just writing that!)

Using plural pronouns to refer to singular antecedents is acceptable in verbal speech or casual notes such as e-mails, but not in professional writing. (See CMOS # 5.46 and AP.)

CMOS #5.225 allows for the use of *he or she* (sparingly). It also lists several techniques for achieving gender neutrality while maintaining proper grammar. To illustrate how these would work, consider the following ways to reword the above sentence:

- Omit the pronoun. ("A writer needs thick skin to work with a professional editor.")

- Repeat the noun. ("A *writer* needs thick skin if that *writer* wants to work with a professional editor.")

- Use a plural antecedent. ("*Writers* need thick skin if *they* want professional editing.")

- Use an article (*a, an, the*) instead of a personal pronoun. ("A writer needs thick skin to work with a professional editor on *a* manuscript.")

- Use the neutral singular pronoun *one*. ("A writer who hires a professional editor needs thicker skin than *one* who doesn't.")

- Use the relative pronoun *who*. ("Thick skin is required of a writer *who* wants to hire a professional editor.")

- Use the imperative mood. ("Get a thick skin if you want to hire a professional editor.")

- Rearrange the sentence. ("Working with a professional editor requires a thick skin.")

I would add two options to the CMOS list:

- Use second-person pronouns. (*"You* need a thick skin if *you* want to work with a professional editor on *your* manuscript." Or *"We* writers need thick skins if *we* want to work with professional editors on *our* manuscripts.")

- Use male pronouns in some sections of your manuscript and female pronouns in other sections. (Just don't use both to refer to the same person!)

6. Match subjects with subjects, objects with objects

Most of the time, the subject pronoun of a phrase or sentence refers to the subject noun of the previous phrase or sentence, while the object pronoun refers to the object noun.

> Stephanie told Nancy about the book signing. Then she told her about the potluck.

> "She" refers to Stephanie (subject), and "her" refers to Nancy (object).

This rule of thumb does not apply if the identity of the pronoun is obvious.

> MaryLynn told Daniel she wouldn't eat caviar. He told her he never ate shellfish.

Subject/Verb Agreement

Make sure the subject and the verb of a sentence agree in number (singular or plural).

The synopsis and sample chapter (two things) *have* to be mailed by Tuesday.

Each proposal (singular) *has* to be mailed separately.

Every contest entry (singular) *has* to be received before the deadline.

None (*not one,* singular) of the stories in that book *is* written in present tense.

When a subject is followed by a phrase that refers to something else, the added phrase does not change the quantity of the original subject.

Terri's bad grammar, as well as her typos, *needs* to be corrected.

The suspenseful plot combined with unexpected twists *makes* this a great book.

Some collective nouns can be treated as either plural or singular, depending on whether you want the focus to be on the unit or on the individual members.

The couple *has* a young daughter.
(Refers to the two people as a single unit.)

The couple *get* along well together.
(Focus is on two individuals; plural "they.")

My family *is* very close.
(Focus is on the unit, which is singular.)

My family *want* the best for me.
(Reference is to several people; plural "they.")

"-Self" Pronouns

Pronouns that end in *-self* are "reflexive pronouns" (*myself, himself, herself, yourself, itself,* and *themselves*). Reflexive pronouns are object pronouns that refer back to the subject of a sentence. (They "reflect" on the subject of the sentence.)

I could see *myself* becoming a best-selling author someday.

Evniki decided to treat *herself* to a nice dinner when she got her first book contract.

The lion cocked its head when it saw *itself* in a mirror.

Use regular object pronouns when the subject and object are different.

The authors who recommend this book are Yvette, Ursula, and *me*.
(You are not "the authors," so *myself* does not work here.)

Reflexive pronouns can also be used to add emphasis to a sentence.

John wrote that book *himself.*

The meaning of the sentence doesn't change if you take out the reflexive pronoun. It just has a different feel because it lacks the added emphasis.

ADD YOUR OWN

My Favorite Pronoun Issues

Pronoun	Problem	Solution

GRAMMAR MYTHS

Generations of English teachers have taught students certain rules that are either personal preferences or rules that have changed over time. Here are a few examples.

Myth #1. Never split an infinitive.
(See CMOS #5.106.)

An "infinitive" is the *to* form of a verb: to go, to talk, to study. "Splitting an infinitive" means to put some word (usually an adverb) between *to* and the verb: to *quickly* go, to *quietly* talk, to *avidly* study.

Rule of thumb: If it's just as easy to word something in a way that avoids splitting an infinitive, do so—if for no better reason than because some readers, editors, and proofreaders will fault you if you don't. However, if doing so interrupts the flow, or makes comprehension difficult or awkward, go ahead and split that infinitive.

Myth #2. Never end a sentence with a preposition.
(See CMOS #5.176.)

A "preposition" is a word that connects with a noun phrase to form a modifying phrase. Most prepositions refer to time, space, or position.

across the country

after the movie

in the room

with ketchup

Many students are taught that prepositions should never come at the end of a sentence. However, the proper ordering of prepositions can sometimes result in sentences that sound awkward, stilted, or pompous.

As a general rule, try to avoid ending sentences with prepositions. But if that's the only way to avoid sounding strange, then by all means, break the rule. Sometimes a preposition is the best word to end a sentence *with*.

Myth #3. Never use the word *hopefully* in place of "It is hoped" or "I/we hope."

Many writers have been upbraided for using what is sometimes considered the colloquial usage of this word. The argument is that *hopefully* means "in a hopeful manner." Therefore, a sentence like "Hopefully, this will clear things up" could only mean "This will clear things up *in a hopeful manner*."

However, according to the latest edition of *Merriam-Webster's Collegiate Dictionary*, *hopefully* has two meanings. The first is "in a hopeful manner." The second is "It is hoped; I hope; we hope." The example given is "Hopefully the rain will end soon."

The second definition of *hopefully* is in a class of adverbs known as "disjuncts." Many other adverbs (*interestingly, frankly, clearly, luckily, unfortunately*) are also disjuncts.

Myth #4. Never start a sentence with a conjunction.
(See CMOS #5.206.)

A "conjunction" is a word that defines the relationship between different units of thought. Examples: *and, so, but, if, or*. Writers are often taught that beginning a sentence with a conjunction makes it incomplete, a sentence fragment. And sometimes that's true. Example:

> Try to catch me. If you can.

But sentence fragments are perfectly acceptable if they're not overused, confusing, or unclear. Experienced writers may deliberately use the occasional sentence fragment for emphasis or to create a particular tone. (Note, however, that a dash can also be used for emphasis, and it is often preferable if the effect is the same.)

In many cases, opening with a conjunction does *not* turn a sentence into a fragment; it simply serves to connect the current information more strongly to the information that comes before it. Beginning a sentence with a conjunction is sometimes the best way to express the sentence's relationship with the previous one.

If you have multiple statements that go together, and then a statement that makes a contrast to the previous ones, make the last statement a separate sentence, starting with "But ..." For example:

> You may not like splitting infinitives. Ending a sentence with a preposition may cause you to cringe. Using *hopefully* to mean "I hope" may be anathema to you. But these are all grammatically correct by today's standards.

If you replaced the period before *but* with a comma, the last statement would refer only to the statement immediately preceding it, rather than to all of the previous statements.

GRAMMAR EXCEPTION

When you write fiction dialogue, you can choose to ignore a lot of grammar rules. Most people don't talk (or think) with proper grammar all the time. As a matter of fact, you might *want* to write certain characters with specific grammatical habits that give the reader insight into their personalities or to identify a character's unique voice. (You probably wouldn't, for example, have a teenager or a country bumpkin or an old-timer or an uneducated orphan using impeccable grammar ... unless there's something special about that character, like his mother is a professional author or editor!)

Even well-educated people often break grammar rules in speech. Most of us use pronouns, for example, based on whether they "sound right." Using the correct pronoun can sometimes make people sound arrogant, as if they are putting on airs. (For example, "To whom do you wish to speak?" is proper, but "Who do you want to talk to?" sounds more natural.)

The trick: Know what the grammar rules are, and only break a rule if you are doing so intentionally with a specific purpose in mind.

ADD YOUR OWN

My Favorite Grammar Rules

Reference Book   Rule or Page #   Rule

Section 5

Spelling

Spelling

The most important advice I can give you about spelling is this:

DO NOT RELY ON SPELL-CHECK!

There are too many mistakes it won't catch, such as "real words" that are not used properly in context. In addition, no spell-check software will have all the spellings in the latest edition of the appropriate dictionary for the type of writing you're doing.

Any word you are unsure of should be looked up. I would advise keeping a list of your own "commonly misspelled words" on a computer file or in this book.

To get you started, here are a few misspelled words I come across often in my editing. Most are "everyday" words, the kind of things you might not think to look up.

COMMONLY MISSPELLED WORDS

Below are some words you might be *positive* you know how to spell, so you may not think to look them up. (My husband's tongue-in-cheek definition of *positive* is "being wrong at the top of your voice.") If you find things here you didn't know, I hope this encourages you to look up the spellings for similar words.

a lot (always two words)

acknowledgment (not *acknowledgement*)

air conditioner (noun—notice, no hyphen)
air-condition (verb)
air-conditioned (adjective)
air-conditioning (noun)
 The AP stylebook says no hyphen in *air conditioning*.

airfare

airmail

all right
 Although most dictionaries list *alright* as a legitimate word, *The Chicago Manual of Style* (#5.220) and the AP stylebook advise never to use that spelling. Many readers consider *alright* to be wrong, but no one has a problem with *all right*. So I recommend avoiding the one-word spelling.

babysat/babysit/babysitter/babysitting
 The AP stylebook has *baby-sat, baby-sit, baby-sitting*, but *baby sitter*.

backyard (one word as either a noun or an adjective)

The AP stylebook spells this as one word (*backyard*) in all uses. However, *Webster's New World College Dictionary,* which the AP stylebook recommends, has one word (*backyard*) when used as a noun, two words (*back yard*) when used as an adjective.

Note that *front yard* is never one word.

barbed wire (not *barb wire*)

bookstore

brainpower

by-product

The AP stylebook has *byproduct.*

cannot

CAT scan (all caps CAT, acronym for Computerized Axial Tomography)

The AP stylebook says the newer term is *CT scan.*

coauthor, coexist, cofounder, coheir, cohost, copartner, copilot, copublish, coruler, cosign, cosponsor, costar, coworker, cowriter, etc.

(However, when the main part of the word following the prefix *co-* starts with an *o,* use a hyphen; e.g., **co-owner.**)

> ### For Articles
>
> The AP stylebook suggests hyphenating *co-* words that indicate occupation or status, such as *co-author, co-host, co-owner, co-partner, co-pilot, co-signer, co-star,* and *co-worker.* However, this is an exception to their recommended *Webster's New World College Dictionary.*

deathbed (noun and adjective)

dining
 I see this spelled with two *n*'s all the time, probably because *dinning* is also a word, so spell-check doesn't catch it.

divorcé (a divorced man)
divorcée (a divorced woman)

> ### For Articles
>
> The AP stylebook has *divorcee* for a woman; no listing for a man who has been divorced. However, its recommended *Webster's New World College Dictionary* has *divorcé* and *divorcée,* with *divorcee* as an alternate spelling for females.

espresso (not *expresso*)

fiancé (a man engaged to be married)
 The AP stylebook has *fiance.*
fiancée (a woman engaged to be married)
 The AP stylebook has *fiancee.*

freelance/freelancer/freelancing

godsend (not capitalized)

Godspeed

good-bye
The AP stylebook has *goodbye*.

handheld (noun and adjective)
The AP stylebook has *handheld* for noun, *hand-held* for adjective.

handmade

harebrained (not *hairbrained*)

homemade (one word, no hyphen)

iced tea (not *ice tea*)

insofar as

ma'am
The AP stylebook prefers *madam*.

makeup (noun or adjective)
make up (verb form)

man-made

midair, midday, midwinter
In general, no hyphen with *mid* unless followed by a capitalized word (mid-America, mid-January) or a figure (mid-30s).

millennium (note two *l*'s and two *n*'s)

mind-set
The AP stylebook has *mindset.*

monthlong

nationwide

newsstand

oceangoing

old-fashioned (not *old fashion,* and always with a hyphen)

oohed/oohing and **aahed/aahing**

predominant/predominantly
(preferred over *predominate* and *predominately*)

rearview mirror
The AP stylebook also lists *sideview* mirror, although their dictionary does not. Webster's Collegiate doesn't list *sideview* either.

restaurateur (not *restauranteur*)

Smithsonian Institution (not *Smithsonian Institute*)

spell-check (noun or verb)
spell-checker or **spelling checker** (noun)
AP and its dictionary have *spell check* (verb); *spell-checker* or *spelling checker* (noun).

straitjacket (not straightjacket)

T-shirt

well-being

Whenever two spellings are given in the dictionary, the first one listed is the preferred spelling. Here are some examples:

amid (not *amidst*)

among (not *amongst*)

backward (not *backwards)*

forward (not *forwards)*

gray (not *grey*)

till (not *'til*)

toward (not *towards)*

ADD YOUR OWN

My Favorite Commonly Misspelled Words

How I Usually Spell It   How It Should Be Spelled

_____

_____

_____

_____

_____

_____

_____

_____

_____

_____

_____

_____

_____

_____

_____

_____

_____

_____

HYPHENATION

The Chicago Manual of Style contains an extensive guide (#7.85) for determining when certain words should be spelled with a hyphen. Here are some examples based on that list.

Compound Modifiers
CMOS #5.91, 7.81–7.84 and AP

As a general rule, a modifying phrase is hyphenated when it's followed by the noun it describes, but not hyphenated when it comes after the noun it modifies.

Adjective + Adjective
"The stove was red hot"
but "a red-hot stove"
(unless the stove was both hot and red, in which case you would write "a red, hot stove" or "a hot, red stove")

Adjective + Noun (or Noun + Adjective)
The manuscript was high quality.
a high-quality manuscript

Writing a novel is time consuming.
a time-consuming project

This computer is user friendly.
a user-friendly software program

Adjective + Participle
The question was open ended.
an open-ended question

Noun + Gerund

(A "gerund" is a noun that expresses generalized or uncompleted action.)

> I love fiction writing.
> a fiction-writing clinic

Noun + Participle

> The novel was suspense filled.
> a suspense-filled novel

Number + Superlative

> His book was fourth to last in the contest.
> the fourth-to-last contestant

> The spine is three inches thick.
> a three-inch-thick spine

Participle + Noun

> Their manuscript was on the cutting edge.
> cutting-edge technology

Participle + Preposition

> This poem is often quoted.
> an often-quoted poem

For Articles

Hyphenate compound modifiers, even if they are not followed by a noun, if they come after a form of "to be." For example: "Fame is often short-lived."

Multiple-Word Modifiers

If an adjective phrase contains multiple words, put hyphens between all of the words in the compound modifier.

> twenty-first-century near-future speculative fiction

> twenty-four-hour-a-day schedule

If two adjective phrases end in a common noun, use a hyphen after each of the unattached words to show that they are both related to the noun.

> This year's schedule includes several three- and four-day clinics.

> This book is targeted for four- to six-year-old children.

Potential Misreading

Occasionally, you may run into a situation where a compound adjective that follows the noun might lead to confusion or ambiguity. For example, "Maureen's book was thought provoking" could mean that her book provoked thought or that it was thought (considered) to be provoking.

If a potential for misreading exists (or the possibility of a distracting, even humorous, secondary interpretation), use a hyphen. Other examples:

> much-loved music ("much loved music" could refer to a lot of loved music)

> less-appreciated art ("less appreciated art" could mean fewer appreciated sketches)

Adverb Phrases
CMOS #5.91, 7.82–7.83, 7.85 and AP

A two-word phrase that begins with an -*ly* adverb is not hyphenated.

a *mildly* worded rejection letter

Amelia's novel has a *highly* developed plot.

Vanessa's heroine felt *utterly* dejected when Roger left her at the altar.

Hyphenate if the -*ly* adverb is part of an adjective phrase.

a not-so-*mildly*-worded rejection letter

Adverb phrases that do *not* end in -*ly* are hyphenated before but not after a noun.

Her book was much loved.
a much-loved book

The man was well read.
a well-read man

Exception: compounds with *most* and *least* are usually open.

Some of the *least* skilled writers in the county entered that contest.

Check *Merriam-Webster's Collegiate Dictionary* for compound adverbs that are always hyphenated, no matter what their usage. For example:

Peggy's husband was long-suffering.

Had Jayna been a long-suffering wife for too many years?

Christ exhibited a spirit of long-suffering we should all emulate.

Unless the dictionary definition contains an example in which the hyphenated modifier is *not* followed by a noun, that should not be taken as an indication that it should always be hyphenated.

Ages

Hyphenate ages in both compound-noun and compound-adjective uses.

My ten-year-old is taking swimming lessons from a seventeen-year-old girl.

Eva babysat a two-and-a-half-year-old child.

Paula's niece is two and a half years old.

Cecilia's teacher is a sixty-five-year-old man.

Brent met a man sixty-five years old.

Brian's class consisted of twenty-four five-year-old boys.

Marlene's son had a party with twenty-four boys five years old.

Colors

CMOS-15 said that color-term compounds in which one word modified another were not hyphenated. CMOS-16, however, says that color-combination modifiers should be hyphenated if followed by a noun.

sea-green scarf

reddish-brown hair

blue-green eyes

black-and-white tile

Norm's tie was cobalt blue.

The bridesmaids' dresses were teal green.

The truth isn't always black and white.

A bouquet of "red and white roses" would consist of some red roses and some white roses. If each rose has both colors in it, you'd have a bouquet of "red-and-white roses."

Numbers

Hyphenated Numbers
CMOS #7.85

Hyphenate numbers twenty-one through ninety-nine.

Simple Fractions
CMOS #9.14

Hyphenate spelled-out fractions, whether they're used as nouns, adjectives, or adverbs (except when the second element is already hyphenated).

one-half; a one-half split

two-thirds; a two-thirds majority

three-quarters; three-quarters done

one twenty-fifth (1/25); a one twenty-fifth share

three fifty-thirds (3/53)

Mixed Fractions
CMOS #9.15

Don't use hyphens when combining whole numbers with hyphenated fractions.

Niki's manuscript was four and one-eighth (4⅛) inches thick.

She wrote for twenty-one and one-quarter (21¼) hours straight.

His second book was two and three-quarters (2¾) as long as his first one.

Note: Quantities consisting of whole numbers and simple fractions may be expressed in numerals instead of being spelled out (especially if a symbol for the fraction is available, as in the examples above).

Compounds with Fractions
CMOS #7.85

Hyphenate adjectives, but not nouns.

Clarissa wrote for a half hour.

After her half-hour session, she ate two pieces of chocolate cake.

For Articles

Hyphenate *half-* fractions in formal writing. In everyday speech, use *a* or *an* after *half*, without a hyphen.

a half-hour; half an hour

a half-mile; half a mile

1 1/2 years (or months or days)

a year (or month or day) and a half

Measurements
CMOS #9.13–9.16

Adjective compounds that have a number and a unit of measure are hyphenated when they come before a noun, not hyphenated when not followed by a noun.

Laura jogged a three-mile path.

Gary's car left a 150-yard skid mark.

Margo's dogs drink two three-ounce bottles of water every day.

Cliff's son scaled a three-meter-high wall.

Penelope climbed a wall three meters high.

When numerals are used and the units are abbreviated, don't use a hyphen even before a noun.

33 m distance

12 kg weight

3 m high wall

3 ft. high statue

1,200 lb. stone

Prefixes and Suffixes

The Chicago Manual of Style has a chart (#7.85) that lists prefixes and suffixes that are commonly combined with other words. It indicates which ones are open, which are hyphenated, and which are closed. Here are a few examples.

all

Most adjective compounds with *all* are hyphenated both before and after a noun.

all-inclusive

all-around

all-powerful

Most adverb compounds with *all* are not hyphenated.

all along

all in

all over

Some depend on whether they come before or after a noun.

"She went all out" but "an all-out war"

cross

Most compounds with *cross* are hyphenated; a few are closed. (If not listed in a dictionary, the compound should be hyphenated.)

cross-referenced

cross-country

crosstown

crosscut

crossover

full

Compound adjectives with *full* are hyphenated before a noun, but not hyphenated after the noun.

full-length mirror

full-time job

Annabel's mirror is full length.

Marcia's drawing is full scale.

Cynthia's job is full time.

like

The suffix *like* is often used to form new compounds. These are usually closed except for words ending in *l* or *ll*, words of three or more syllables, compound words, most proper nouns, or other forms that might be difficult to read. When in doubt, hyphenate.

childlike

sail-like

vacuum-bottle-like

Whitman-like

Christlike

For Articles

Do not put a hyphen before the suffix *like* unless not doing so would cause the letter *l* to be tripled (*bill-like, shell-like*) or unless the main element is a proper noun (*Norwalk-like*).

They make an exception for *flu-like,* but not *Christlike.*

---

over, under

Adjectives with the prefix *over* or *under* are closed unless they are multiple-word modifiers containing *the*, in which case they are hyphenated.

> overexposed, overrated, underhanded

> over-the-counter, under-the-table

self

Most adjectives with *self* are hyphenated. When the additional prefix *un* is used, close the compound. When *self* is added to a suffix, the word is closed.

> self-reliant, self-sustaining, self-righteous, self-confident, self-conscious

> unselfconscious

> selfless, selfish

well, ill, better, best, little, lesser, least

Compounds with adjectives or participles are hyphenated before the noun, open after a noun, and open if modified by an adverb.

> He was well known.
> a well-known author

> She was better prepared for her second meeting with the publisher than she was the first time.
> She's a better-prepared writer.

Common Phrases

Some popular expressions use hyphens. For example, Webster's Collegiate lists *24-7* for twenty-four hours a day, seven days a week. (But the AP stylebook uses a slash: 24/7.)

Stuttering/Stammering

Hyphens are used to designate stuttering or stammering in dialogue when a character is frightened or cold, or has a speech impediment. (Note: I've found no rule for this in *The Chicago Manual of Style,* but it is common practice in published fiction and is addressed in the CMOS online forum.)

> B-b-but I don't w-want to s-sing in p-public.

> R-Rachel? Did you see that m-m-monster?

Use an em dash for a longer pause if the speaker is trying to figure out what to say or is caught off guard.

> I—I don't know what to say.

As with most things of this nature, use this device sparingly so as not to irritate readers.

ADD YOUR OWN

My Favorite Hyphenation Rules

Correct Spelling   Definition/Usage

SLANG

Some slang words are listed in the industry-standard dictionaries, so look up words like these if you want to use them. Here are some examples. (In parentheses I've noted which dictionary lists the word: MWC for *Merriam-Webster's Collegiate Dictionary*; NWC for *Webster's New World College Dictionary*.) These words are commonly found in commercially published books (especially novels)—even those that are only listed in AP's dictionary.

aha: used to express surprise, triumph, or derision (MWC)

> *Aha!* I finally found a good book about proofreading.

c'mon: abbreviation for "come on" (NWC)

> *C'mon*, let's go!

gimme: informal pronunciation for "give me" (NWC)

> *Gimme* a break!

gonna: informal pronunciation for "going to" (NWC)

> I'm *gonna* go now.

gotta: informal pronunciation for "got to" (NWC)

> I've *gotta* learn how to do this right.

ha-ha: used to express amusement or derision (MWC and NWC)

Very funny, Joe. *Ha-ha.*

huh: used to express surprise, disbelief, or confusion; or as an inquiry inviting affirmative reply (MWC)

> "*Huh,*" Wayne said as he stared at the confusing lesson in Katie's workbook.

> "*Huh!*" Gordon muttered. "I never knew about that spelling rule."

> "*Huh?*" Cari asked, certain she couldn't possibly have heard Jacob correctly.

li'l: abbreviation for "little" (MWC)

> Give Mommy a kiss, you sweet *li'l* girl.

sh: used to urge or command silence or less noise (MWC and NWC)

> "*Sh,*" Miranda cautioned. "Alexander's in the next room!"

Note: Both dictionaries say the pronunciation is "often prolonged," so no need to add more *h*'s.

uh-huh: used to indicate affirmation, agreement, or gratification; slang for "yes" (MWC and NWC)

> "*Uh-huh,*" Dustin said, nodding. "That's exactly what I said."

uh-uh: used to indicate negation; slang for "no" (MWC and NWC)

"Uh-uh," Max replied. "I will not do that, no matter what Edwina says."

wanna: informal pronunciation for "want to" (NWC)

I *wanna* be a best-selling author.

wannabe: a person who aspires to be someone or something else, or who tries to look or act like someone else (MWC and NWC)

She wrote like a Danielle Steele *wannabe.*

That writers' conference is great for *wannabes.*

y'all: contraction for "you all" (MWC and NWC)

"Y'all want to watch *Gone With the Wind* tonight?" Joyce asked.

yea: slang for "yippee" or "hooray"

The MWC definitions for *yea* refer only to affirmative statements or votes. (Examples: "Did you vote *yea* or nay?" and *"Yea,* when this flesh and heart shall fail, and mortal life shall cease ..." from "Amazing Grace.") However, the same pronunciation is often used in informal speech to express exuberant delight or triumph (*yippee*) or joy/approval/encouragement (*hooray*). And NWC allows for the use of *yea* as a cheer. (Note: *Yay* is not listed in either of the industry-standard dictionaries, so don't use that spelling.)

yeah: colloquial form of *yes* (MWC and NWC)

"Well, *yeah,* of course I'll marry you," Lizzy told Gene.

For Articles

The AP stylebook says, "Do not use substandard spellings such as *gonna* or *wanna* in attempts to convey regional dialects or informal pronunciations, except to help a desired touch or to convey an emphasis by the speaker."

SOUND WORDS

Many words that describe sounds are in the dictionary. Here are a few examples:

cheep: a faint, shrill sound

thunk: a flat, hollow sound

thwack: the sound of a heavy blow

tsk: a "dental click" used to express disapproval
   (Note: *Tsk-tsk* is a verb, as in "Why did you *tsk-tsk* me?")

whack: the sound of a resounding blow

whoosh: the sound created by a swift or explosive rush

If a word is listed in the industry-standard dictionary, do not put it in italics. But if you make up a word to describe a sound and it's not in the dictionary, put that word in italics.

ADD YOUR OWN

My Favorite Slang/Sound Words that *Are* in the Dictionary

How Webster's Spells It   Definition

_____

_____

_____

_____

_____

_____

_____

My Favorite Slang/Sound Words that *Aren't* in the Dictionary

How I Spell It   What It Means to Me

_____

_____

_____

_____

_____

_____

_____

_____

_____

TERMS FOR MODERN TECHNOLOGY

The Internet has been around for years now. But the "experts" are still figuring out how to spell words associated with it. Below are a few examples of what the most recent editions of the industry-standard references show.

Note: In this section, I use MWC for *Merriam-Webster's Collegiate Dictionary* (the one recommended by *The Chicago Manual of Style,* for books and popular-style magazines) and NWC for *Webster's New World College Dictionary* (the one recommended by *The Associated Press Stylebook,* for newspapers and journalistic-style magazines).

e-book, e-reader

All four sources have *e-book* lowercased with a hyphen.

NWC does not have a listing for *e-reader,* but all other sources have it lowercased with a hyphen.

e-mail

This word is lowercased and hyphenated in CMOS, MWC, and NWC.

The most recent AP has taken out the hyphen. (However, AP retains the hyphen in all other "e-words," such as *e-business* and *e-commerce.*)

Internet (aka the Net)

Always capitalize Internet.

CMOS (7.76) has *the net* lowercased. Their dictionary, MWC, says the *net* is "often capitalized."

AP capitalizes *the Net*. Their dictionary, NWC, says it's "usually" capitalized.

log on/logon

Log on is a verb phrase, meaning "to enter the necessary information to begin a session on a computer or network" (aka *log in*). *Log off* refers to entering the necessary information to end the session.

Logon is a noun, referring to the procedure used to get access to an operating system or application, usually requiring a user ID and password (aka *login*). Note: NWC does not have an entry for *login* or *logon*.

online

All four sources spell this as one word (no hyphen) when used as an adjective or adverb.

> an *online* database

> I'm shopping *online* right now.

web page

CMOS has *web page*. MWC does not have a separate listing for this word; however, since they capitalize *Web*, *Web page* would be capitalized as well.

AP and NWC have *Web page*.

website

MWC has *Web site*, but all other sources have *website*.

World Wide Web (aka the Web)

The World Wide Web (always capitalized) is not the same as the Internet. Webster's Collegiate defines the Internet as "an electronic communications network that connects computer networks and organizational computer facilities around the world." The Web is "a part of the Internet accessed through a graphical user interface and containing documents often connected by hyperlinks."

CMOS lowercases *the web*. But their dictionary, MWC, capitalizes *the Web*.

AP has *the Web*. Their dictionary, NWC, says *the Web* is "usually" capitalized.

other "web" words

MWC has *webcam, webcast, webmaster*. (CMOS does not give spellings for these words.)

AP has *Web feed*. (NWC does not have listings for any Web terms other than *the Web, Web page, and website*.)

Dictionaries always change some spellings in each new edition, especially with technology terms. So make sure you always consult the most recent version.

When there's a discrepancy between a style guide and its recommended dictionary, you could make a case for either spelling. Most publishers will have in-house guidelines that cover these issues. Without that, a good rule of thumb would be to go by whichever reference was published most recently. For example, the 2010 edition of *The Chicago Manual of Style* would supersede the 2003 edition of *Merriam-Webster's Collegiate Dictionary*. And the most recent edition of *The Associated Press Stylebook* (especially if you use the online version, which is regularly updated) would supersede the printed dictionary.

ADD YOUR OWN

My Favorite Modern-Technology Terms

Term   Definition

TRADEMARKS

Many generic-sounding words are actually trademarked brand names. Most trademarked words aren't off-limits for writers, as long as you double-check the spelling and use proper capitalization. However, the International Trademark Association has a list of rules for using trademark names. Here are a few:

1. NEVER (*yes, they use all caps*) use a trademark as a noun, only an adjective. (They want to see "Kleenex tissues," not just "Kleenex.")

2. NEVER use a trademark as a verb, only an adjective. (No *xeroxing*, only "photocopying on a Xerox copier.")

3. NEVER make a trademark name plural. (No OREOS or LEGOs or Rollerblades.)

4. NEVER make a trademark name possessive—unless the trademark itself is possessive. (For example, "Levi's jeans" is okay, but not "the Jet Ski's motor.")

Most publishers prefer generic equivalents unless the trademark name is essential.

Here are a few examples of trademarked words (with their generic equivalents in parentheses):

Band-Aid (adhesive bandage)

Bubble Wrap (air-filled plastic packaging material)

ChapStick (lip balm)

Coca-Cola/Coke (cola, soda, or pop, depending on the area of the country)

Crock-Pot (slow cooker)

Dumpster (trash bin, waste receptacle, garbage container)
  The latest AP has *dumpster* as a generic term.

Frisbee (toy flying saucer)

Hula-Hoop (plastic toy hoop)

Jacuzzi (whirlpool, spa, therapeutic whirlpool bath)

Jaws of Life (tool to pry open a vehicle to free people trapped inside)

Jell-O (gelatin or pudding)

Jet Ski (personal watercraft, recreational watercraft)

Jetway (passenger ramp between a terminal building and an aircraft)

Kitty Litter (cat box filler)

Kmart (discount store)

La-Z-Boy (recliner)

Laundromat (self-service laundry)

Ping-Pong (table tennis)

Post-it Note (sticky note)

Q-tip (cotton swab)

Scotch tape (transparent adhesive tape)

Silly Putty (modeling clay)

Styrofoam (insulation)
Note: Styrofoam is an extruded polystyrene foam made for thermal insulation. Contrary to popular use, disposable cups are not made of this material.

Teflon (nonstick coating)

Walmart (discount retail store)
Note: The corporate name is "Wal-Mart Stores Inc."

Windbreaker (lightweight jacket)

Note: CMOS #8.152 says there is no legal requirement to use trademark symbols (® and ™) in books, either fiction or nonfiction, and those symbols should be omitted wherever possible. However, if your publisher requires them, they should appear *before* any period, comma, or other punctuation mark.

PUBLISHERS' PREFERENCES

Most, if not all, publishers have their own in-house lists of spelling preferences. Until you've started working for a specific company, it's best to follow the industry-standard guidelines. (No publisher will mind changing industry-standard spellings to their in-house spellings.)

However, there's one word that seems to be on most publishers' exceptions list.

OK vs. okay

Merriam-Webster's Collegiate Dictionary lists *OK* as the standard spelling, with *okay* as a "variant." However, most book publishers prefer *okay* (possibly to avoid confusion with the abbreviation for Oklahoma, or maybe just because the all-caps spelling tends to jump off the page and bring attention to itself.)

If you're working with a particular house, find out what their preference is and use that. If not, either spelling is...well, *acceptable*.

Since more publishers seem to like *okay*, that's the spelling I use (except when I'm sending something to a publisher whose known preference is *OK*).

For Articles

The AP stylebook says to always use *OK*, not *okay*.

Just *never* spell this word as "ok"!

INTERESTING QUOTE

Many cultures believed the letters of their alphabets were far more than just symbols for communication, recording transactions, or recalling history. They believed letters were powerful magical symbols that could be used to cast spells and predict the future. The Norse runes and the Hebrew alphabet are simple letters for spelling words, but also deep symbols of cosmic significance. This magical sense is preserved in our word *spelling*. When you "spell" a word correctly, you are in effect casting a spell, charging these abstract, arbitrary symbols with meaning and power.[2]

---

[2] Christopher Vogler, *The Writer's Journey* (Pan Books, 1999), 298.

CONCLUSION

I hope you enjoy *Proofreading Secrets of Best-Selling Authors*. If you'd like an autographed copy of this book, just send an e-mail request to Kathy@KathyIde.com.

I also speak at writers' conferences on this topic (and others). Let me know if you'd be interested in having me on faculty for your event.

If you'd like some one-on-one, hands-on help with your manuscript (or even just a few chapters of it), please e-mail me. I do all levels of editing, from mentoring aspiring authors through final proofreading before a manuscript is printed. I offer a $5/hour discount on my standard hourly rate to anyone who has purchased this book.

If I'm not the right editor for you, I can help find the right one for you. I am the founder and director of the Christian Editor Connection (www.ChristianEditor.com), which refers authors, agents, and publishers to established, professional Christian freelance editors. We offer a full range of editorial services, including flat-rate overall critiques of book proposals, sample chapters, and complete manuscripts. (If you're a freelance editor looking for more jobs that fit your specific background, qualifications, and specialties, please fill out the online application.)

If you are an editorial freelancer, or think you may be interested in becoming one, I can help you get connected with people like you. I am the founder and director of The Christian PEN: Proofreaders and Editors Network (www.TheChristianPEN.com). This professional support organization offers great tips and articles on the website, an e-mail discussion loop, online courses, job leads, editor mentoring, and more.

Happy proofreading!

Kathy Ide
www.KathyIde.com

APPENDIX A

When books of the Bible are abbreviated, use the following abbreviations (per CMOS #10.47–10.50 and CWMS p. 20). The first column is for popular-style books (including devotionals and most Bible studies). The second column should only be used in scholarly or technical works. (Note the periods in the abbreviations in the first column; no periods in the second column.)

Title of Book	General Style	Scholarly Style
Old Testament		
Genesis	Gen.	Ge
Exodus	Ex.	Ex
Leviticus	Lev.	Lev
Numbers	Num.	Nu
Deuteronomy	Deut.	Dt
Joshua	Josh.	Jos
Judges	Judg.	Jdg
Ruth	Ruth	Ru
1 Samuel	1 Sam.	1Sa
2 Samuel	2 Sam.	2Sa
1 Kings	1 Kings	1Ki
2 Kings	2 Kings	2Ki
1 Chronicles	1 Chron.	1Ch
2 Chronicles	2 Chron.	2Ch
Ezra	Ezra	Ezr

Nehemiah	Neh.	Ne
Esther	Est.	Est
Job	Job	Job
Psalm(s)	Ps. (Pss.)	Ps(s)
Proverbs	Prov.	Pr
Ecclesiastes	Eccl.	Ecc
Song of Songs/Solomon	Song	SS
Isaiah	Isa.	Isa
Jeremiah	Jer.	Jer
Lamentations	Lam.	La
Ezekiel	Ezek.	Eze
Daniel	Dan.	Da
Hosea	Hos.	Hos
Joel	Joel	Joel
Amos	Amos	Am
Obadiah	Obad.	Ob
Jonah	Jonah	Jnh
Micah	Mic.	Mic
Nahum	Nah.	Na
Habakkuk	Hab.	Hab
Zephaniah	Zeph.	Zep
Haggai	Hag.	Hag
Zechariah	Zech.	Zec
Malachi	Mal.	Mal

New Testament

Matthew	Matt.	Mt
Mark	Mark	Mk
Luke	Luke	Lk
John	John	Jn
Acts	Acts	Ac
Romans	Rom.	Ro
1 Corinthians	1 Cor.	1Co
2 Corinthians	2 Cor.	2Co
Galatians	Gal.	Gal
Ephesians	Eph.	Eph
Philippians	Phil.	Php
Colossians	Col.	Col
1 Thessalonians	1 Thess.	1Th
2 Thessalonians	2 Thess.	2Th
1 Timothy	1 Tim.	1Ti
2 Timothy	2 Tim.	2Ti
Titus	Titus	Tit
Philemon	Philem.	Phm
Hebrews	Heb.	Heb
James	James	Jas
1 Peter	1 Peter	1Pe
2 Peter	2 Peter	2Pe
1 John	1 John	1Jn

2 John	2 John	2Jn
3 John	3 John	3Jn
Jude	Jude	Jude
Revelation	Rev.	Rev

APPENDIX B

Proofreading tips in this book were graciously provided by the following best-selling authors (listed in alphabetical order by last name).

Lisa Tawn Bergren (http://lisatawnbergren.com) is the best-selling, award-winning author of more than thirty books, with more than 1.5 million copies sold.

Renae Brumbaugh (www.RenaeBrumbaugh.com) is a two-time best-selling author and award-winning journalist.

Wanda E. Brunstetter (www.wandabrunstetter.com) is an award-winning author of more than sixty books, with more than six million copies sold. Many of her books have landed on several best-seller lists, including *The New York Times, Publisher's Weekly, CBA, ECPA,* and *CBD.* Her work has been covered by national publications, including *Time* magazine and *USA Today.*

Mary DeMuth (www.marydemuth.com) is the author of twelve books, both fiction and nonfiction. She also has an active speaking and mentoring ministry.

Lena Nelson Dooley (www.lenanelsondooley.com) has more than 700,000 books in print. She is a frequent speaker at women's groups, writers' groups, and regional and national conferences. She is one of the cohosts of the *Gate Beautiful* blog radio show. American Christian Fiction Writers awarded her the Mentor of the Year Award in 2006, and she has been a frequent finalist.

Suzanne Woods Fisher (www.suzannewoodsfisher.com) is the author of more than fifteen books, fiction and nonfiction, for Revell Books. She has been a Carol Award winner and a finalist for the Christy Award and ECPA's Book of Year.

Anita Higman (www.anitahigman.com) is the award-winning author of thirty-four books (several coauthored) for adults and children. She's been a Barnes & Noble "Author of the Month" for Houston and has a BA in the combined fields of speech communication, psychology, and art.

Randy Ingermanson (www.ingermanson.com) has published six novels (some coauthored) and two nonfiction books, including *Writing Fiction for Dummies*. His first book, *Who Wrote the Bible Code?*, won Best Book Published in 1999 by the San Diego Christian Writers' Guild. His novels have won the Christy, the Silver Angel, and other awards.

Kathi Macias (www.kathimacias.com) is a multi-award-winning writer who has authored more than forty books and ghostwritten several others. A former newspaper columnist and string reporter, Kathi has taught creative and business writing in various venues and has been a guest on many radio and television programs.

Gail Gaymer Martin (www.gailgaymermartin.com) writes Christian fiction for Love Inspired and Barbour Publishing. She has fifty-two contracted novels with more than three and a half million books in print. She is the author of Writers Digest's *Writing the Christian Romance*. Gail is a cofounder and executive board member of American Christian Fiction Writers, a member of the Christian Authors Network, and a keynote speaker at churches, libraries, and civic organizations.

Susan Meissner (www.susanmeissner.com) is a multi-published author, speaker, and writing workshop leader with a background in community journalism. Her novels include *The Shape of Mercy*, named by Publishers Weekly as one of the 100 Best Novels of 2008, and a Carol Award winner.

Deborah Raney (www.deborahraney.com) has authored more than twenty books, including *A Vow to Cherish*, which inspired the World Wide Pictures film of the same title. Her books have won the RITA Award, ACFW's Carol Award, the HOLT Medallion, National Readers' Choice Award, and the Silver Angel, and have twice been Christy Award finalists.

Gayle Roper (www.gayleroper.com) has published more than forty books. She has been a Christy Award finalist three times, won the Holt Medallion three times, and has won the Romance Writers of America's RITA Award for Best Inspirational Romance, the Reviewers Choice Award, the Award of Excellence, the Golden Quill, and the Romantic Times Lifetime Achievement Award.

Lynette Sowell (www.facebook.com/lynettesowellauthor) is the award-winning author of more than a dozen titles for Barbour Publishing. In 2009, Lynette was voted one of the favorite new authors by Heartsong Presents book club readers. Her historical romance, *All That Glitters*, was a finalist in ACFW's 2010 Carol Awards. She loves reading, cooking, watching movies, and Texas road trips.

Kay Marshall Strom (www.kaystrom.com) is the award-winning author of forty-two books. Her writing includes numerous magazine articles, curriculum, and movie scripts. Well established as a nonfiction writer, her latest six books have been fiction. In addition to her writing, Kay is an in-demand speaker.

Cindy Woodsmall (www.cindywoodsmall.com) is a *New York Times* best-selling author who has written a dozen works of fiction and one nonfiction. Cindy has been featured on *ABC Nightline* and the front page of *The Wall Street Journal,* and she worked with National Geographic on a documentary concerning Amish life. In June of 2013, *The Wall Street Journal* listed Cindy as the second most popular author of Amish fiction, following Beverly Lewis. She's won Fiction Book of the Year, Reviewer's Choice Awards, the Inspirational Reader's Choice Contest, and Crossings' Best Book of the Year. She's been a finalist for the prestigious Christy, Rita, and Carol Awards, Christian Book of the Year, and Christian Retailers Choice Awards.

Made in the USA
Columbia, SC
15 May 2020